# Equal Rights to the Curriculum

**PARENTS' and TEACHERS' GUIDES**
**Series Editor:** Professor Colin Baker, *University of Wales, Bangor, Wales, Great Britain*

A Parents' and Teachers' Guide to Bilingualism (3rd edn)
  *Colin Baker*
Second Language Students in Mainstream Classrooms
  *Coreen Sears*
Dyslexia: A Parents' and Teachers' Guide
  *Trevor Payne and Elizabeth Turner*
The Care and Education of a Deaf Child: A Book for Parents
  *Pamela Knight and Ruth Swanwick*
Guía para padres y maestros de niños bilingües
  *Alma Flor Ada and Colin Baker*
Making Sense in Sign: A Lifeline for a Deaf Child
  *Jenny Froude*
Language Strategies for Bilingual Families
  *Suzanne Barron-Hauwaert*
Bilingualism in International Schools: A Model for Enriching Language Education
  *Maurice Carder*

**Other Books of Interest**
Bilingual Children's Language and Literacy Development
  *Roger Barnard and Ted Glynn (eds)*
Bilingual Education: An Introductory Reader
  *Ofelia García and Colin Baker (eds)*
Childhood Bilingualism: Research on Infancy through School Age
  *Peggy McCardle and Erika Hoff (eds)*
Developing in Two Languages: Korean Children in America
  *Sarah J. Shin*
Foundations of Bilingual Education and Bilingualism (4th edn)
  *Colin Baker*
Imagining Multilingual Schools: Language in Education and Glocalization
  *Ofelia García, Tove Skutnabb-Kangas and María Torres-Guzmán (eds)*
Language and Identity in a Dual Immersion School
  *Kim Potowski*
Language and Literacy in Bilingual Children
  *D. Kimbrough Oller and Rebecca E. Eilers (eds)*
A Portrait of the Young in the New Multilingual Spain
  *Carmen Pérez-Vidal, Maria Juan-Garau and Aurora Bel (eds)*
Raising Bilingual-Biliterate Children in Monolingual Cultures
  *Stephen J. Caldas*
Teacher Collaboration and Talk in Multilingual Classrooms
  *Angela Creese*
Teaching English as an International Language: Identity, Resistance and Negotiation
  *Phan Le Ha*
Three is a Crowd? Acquiring Portuguese in a Trilingual Environment
  *Madalena Cruz-Ferreira*
Understanding Deaf Culture: In Search of Deafhood
  *Paddy Ladd*

**For more details of these or any other of our publications, please contact:**
**Multilingual Matters, Frankfurt Lodge, Clevedon Hall,**
**Victoria Road, Clevedon, BS21 7HH, England**
**http://www.multilingual-matters.com**

**PARENTS' AND TEACHERS' GUIDES 10**
*Series Editor:* Colin Baker

# Equal Rights
# to the Curriculum
## Many Languages, One Message

Eithne Gallagher

**MULTILINGUAL MATTERS**
Clevedon • Buffalo • Toronto

**Library of Congress Cataloging in Publication Data**
Gallagher, Eithne
Equal Rights to the Curriculum: Many Languages, One Message / Eithne Gallagher.
Parents' and Teachers' Guides: 10
Includes bibliographical references and index.
1. Students, Foreign–Education. 2. International schools–Curricula. 3. English language–Study and teaching–Foreign speakers 4. School choice. I. Title.
LC3719.G35 2008
371.826'91–dc22             2008000299

**British Library Cataloguing in Publication Data**
A catalogue entry for this book is available from the British Library.

ISBN-13: 978-1-84769-068-5 (hbk)
ISBN-13: 978-1-84769-067-8 (pbk)

**Multilingual Matters**
*UK*: Frankfurt Lodge, Clevedon Hall, Victoria Road, Clevedon BS21 7HH.
*USA*: UTP, 2250 Military Road, Tonawanda, NY 14150, USA.
*Canada*: UTP, 5201 Dufferin Street, North York, Ontario M3H 5T8, Canada.

The policy of Multilingual Matters/Channel View Publications is to use papers that are natural, renewable and recyclable products, made from wood grown in sustainable forests. In the manufacturing process of our books, and to further support our policy, preference is given to printers that have FSC and PEFC Chain of Custody certification. The FSC and/or PEFC logos will appear on those books where full certification has been granted to the printer concerned.

Typeset by Archetype-IT Ltd (http://www.archetype-it.com).
Printed and bound in Great Britain by the Cromwell Press Ltd.

# Contents

# Acknowledgements

I would like to thank all those children, parents and teachers who have shared their stories with me over the past 20 years. I am particularly indebted to teachers who wrote to me in my role as committee member and then later as Chair of the European Council of International Schools (ECIS) ESL and Mother-Tongue Committee, voicing their concerns, many of which are included in the text as case studies.

A thousand thanks go to Aimee Fenneman, Laura Lo Bianco, Rachel Rossi and Sue Reid, my teacher colleagues, who have read all the chapters in their various stages and offered both encouragement and advice.

Much appreciation is due to everyone I have worked with on the ECIS ESL&MT committee over the past ten years. I would particularly like to thank Maurice Carder, John Deighan, Kim Oppenheim, Lyndi Readdean and Pat Mertin who read and commented on various chapters of the book.

I'd like to thank Brian Dare for answering all my queries on Systemic Functional Linguistics over the years and also the South Australian Department of Education & Children's Services for allowing me to adapt their teaching notes on Genre from *ESL in the Mainstream* in Figure 8.

Thank you to Kevin Bartlett for reading and commenting on the chapters and for writing about the International School of Brussels in Chapter 1 and also to Terry Haywood for reading various chapters and offering valuable advice.

I am indebted to Mike Allan, not only for a great Sunday lunch in the oldest pub in Wales, but also for an entertaining discussion on Internationalism and for allowing me to reproduce his Internationalism Audit material in the appendix of this book.

A big thank you must go to Sr. Anne Marie Hill, Director of the Network of Schools for the Sacred Heart of Mary, for allowing me time and encouraging me to give workshops and presentations. The same is due to Dixie McKay CEO of the European Council of International Schools for her encouragement and support.

I'm grateful to Marjukka Grover of Multilingual Matters for the keen interest and support she has shown in this project from the very beginning, for her understanding when I missed yet another deadline and for answering my many questions always with enthusiasm.

I owe a huge vote of thanks to Edna Murphy. Edna published my first article and has encouraged me to write ever since. She has read and commented on every page of this book. Edna is the kind of administrator I dream of working with. She made ESL a priority in the schools she ran and had the foresight way back in 1990 to produce a handbook on ESL for teachers and administrators in International Schools. I thank her for sharing her wisdom with me and also for her friendship.

I would like to thank Colin Baker for doing his best to teach me not to preach, for his editorial guidance, encouraging comments, his enthusiasm for my work and for allowing me to use his glossary.

This book would not exist without the work of Jim Cummins. I first read his work over 25 years ago and I have been inspired by it ever since. I feel both honoured and privileged to have worked with him over the past 12 years. I thank him for his valuable time and detailed comments. He has in many ways helped shape this book.

My three bilingual children Conor, Tess and Aisling helped me to think not only as a teacher but also as a parent. I thank them for their typing, our many animated discussions on education and, above all, for their patience. A special thank you goes to Tess for designing the cover illustration and capturing the book's essential concept so beautifully.

Lastly, my husband Barry Deeks deserves a great deal of thanks for putting up with me! He has read and commented on the book, taken my simple drawings and notes and turned them into clear diagrams and figures, assumed the role of my personal assistant, fed me and the family and understood when I locked myself away to work. I thank him for his love and patience.

# *Foreword*

*Equal Rights to the Curriculum: Many Languages, One Message* is all about transforming knowledge into action. It provides parents with the research-based information necessary to envision their children's full potential as human beings – who they can become and what they are capable of achieving – together with the tools to collaborate on an equal basis with their children's teachers to bring this vision closer to realisation. Likewise, for educators, this book opens up identity spaces – it provides an opportunity to reflect on the kinds of interactions we orchestrate in our classrooms, the messages we convey to students about their past and their future, and the extent to which we are expanding rather than constricting our students' identity options. It challenges us to rethink why we have become educators and what we are capable of achieving as educators. Eithne Gallagher invites us to reclaim agency – the power to act – in our professional lives, by advocating for the kinds of change that will transform our schools into everything implied by the term *international* – environments that promote vigorous intellectual inquiry and that cultivate equitable and respectful communication across languages, cultures and religions.

This book is also about *authority*. The noun gives rise to two very different adjectives – *authoritarian* and *authoritative*. We use the term 'authoritarian' to describe leaders who demand obedience and submission regardless of the veracity or legitimacy of their decisions; policy and practice are determined by ideology – preformed ideas-rather than by research; this style of leadership has little use for dialogue and collaboration. The term 'authoritative', on the other hand, refers to individuals whose perspectives or claims generate respect because they are the result of thoughtful inquiry and are backed up by convincing evidence. The pages of human history, as well as the history of educational institutions, are filled with examples of both kinds of leadership. A central message in *Equal Rights to the Curriculum* is that educators have the opportunity and ethical responsibility to become authoritative in their area of expertise – teaching. We shape the intellectual and social futures of the children in our classrooms – we need to know what we are doing. Collaboratively with our colleagues we need to expand our expertise so that we become confident and competent in teaching students who are learning the school language and whose cultural experiences may be very different from our own.

This book provides a wealth of research-based information about what is good for children in International Schools. It wraps this information around the lives and experiences of administrators, teachers, parents and children who are interacting on a daily basis in schools around the world. We emerge from the pages of this book armed with authoritative knowledge, inspired by the insight that education is an act of imagination that we can, and must, influence, and empowered to take action to change mindsets and organisational structures that limit children's academic and intellectual development. As Eithne Gallagher reminds us, part of our ethical responsibility as educators is to challenge misinformed leaders whose decisions are authoritarian rather than authoritative. As parents, we are also in a position to challenge teachers who may be misinformed about what is good for our children.

We have all been misinformed at various times as parents, teachers and educational leaders. In an era of rapidly changing educational realities that reflect our mutating societies, no one has all the answers. But all of us can search for better information and for more effective teaching strategies to achieve our educational goals. Authoritarian leadership, or teaching, or parenting, is the refusal to become a learner. In the context of both International Schools and public schools serving increasingly diverse students and communities, authoritarian leaders demand conformity to past traditions of linguistic and cultural privilege. They also refuse to imagine alternative social orders based on equity of language and culture and acknowledgement of diversity as a crucial global resource.

The limitations of authoritarian styles of leadership are becoming increasingly clear. Fortunately, a major shift in perspective is taking place within the International Schools community. There is increasing recognition that students for whom English is a second (or third) language (ESL) are the norm and that these students do not suffer from intrinsic deficits by virtue of the fact that English is not their home language. For many years, policy and practice in International Schools was as likely to position students' multilingualism as a deficit rather than an asset.

International Schools are the scouting parties of educational globalisation. At a time when population mobility and cross-cultural contact are at an all-time high in human history, International Schools are in the vanguard of exploring uncharted territory. Education as a societal institution was originally established to reinforce conformity among homogeneous populations and to promote homogeneity among diverse populations. It is no exaggeration to say that human survival may depend on how successfully we can navigate to a new educational paradigm. Resolution of urgent ecological challenges and mediation of global conflicts require cooperation rather than competition, respect rather than disdain, and the exercise of imaginative intellect rather than conventional thinking.

Many English-medium International Schools are beginning to move away from unquestioned use of English as the only legitimate language of instruction and interaction within the school. Gradually, other languages are being acknowledged as important cognitive tools, as crucial channels of communication within the family, and as resources for communication and cooperation within our global community. However, for many schools this journey is just beginning and some have not even realised the dysfunctional and discriminatory nature of 'education as usual'.

Eithne Gallagher's book has the potential to jumpstart this process. It maps the landscape and invites dialogue about how best to proceed. Different schools will, and should, pursue different directions. This is intrinsic to teacher agency. The choices we make are infused with challenge, opportunity and responsibility. Some schools will place more emphasis on exploring transformative pedagogies – enabling students to see themselves as change agents who are capable of influencing the negotiation and distribution of power in their worlds; others will encourage students to use their home languages as cognitive tools and support them in transferring concepts and learning strategies across languages – what Eithne Gallagher calls *interlingual teaching*. Still others will focus on instilling an international orientation across the curriculum where mathematics, science, literature and social studies draw from a global knowledge base rather than privileging only Western orientations to knowledge. Clearly, all of these pedagogical directions will reinforce each other.

Hopefully, educators within International Schools will document these initiatives so that they will illuminate new possibilities for addressing linguistic and cultural diversity within the public education systems in many countries. Diversity is still perceived all too often as part of the problem rather than as part of the solution. The classroom examples presented in this book illustrate vividly the opportunities for intellectual enrichment that open up when we welcome children's cultural experiences, and the languages in which these experiences are encoded, into the instructional space.

As I read Eithne Gallagher's book, it rekindled a memory from almost 30 years ago. I remember listening to Mary Ashworth's closing address to the Ontario Teachers of English as a Second Language conference in Toronto in the late 1970s. Mary, an iconic figure and perhaps the most influential pioneer of ESL in Canada, drew our attention to the fact that many second generation newcomer children came to school bilingual, or soon-to-be-bilingual, but left school 12 years later essentially monolingual in English, having lost their fluency in their home languages. She pointed out that when schools were complicit in this process, either through hostility towards or benign neglect of children's home languages, they negated the core meaning of the term *education*, which refers to the process of nourishing talents and expanding potential. Eithne Gallagher likewise invites us to nourish students' talents, including their multilingual talents, and to expand their potential to act effectively and powerfully in their personal lives and on the global stage.

Jim Cummins
Toronto
January 2008

# *Introduction*

In writing this book I had two main audiences in mind, parents and educators:

- Parents of second language children, parents of bilingual children and parents who have children in the many International Schools around the world.
- Educators: ESL teachers, mainstream teachers and administrators who work in International Education.

The book provides an introductory text for those interested in learning about the world of International Education and the important role that second language plays within it. However, the text is not restricted only to the world of privately run International Schools. Schools in every part of our globe are becoming international through necessity as they awaken to the reality of having to deal with culturally diverse children. This book therefore aims to contribute to the skills and understanding of teacher trainers, teachers, administrators and policy makers whose concern is to provide for the educational needs of *all* children growing up in a multicultural society. The book will also be of value to parents who need to choose the right school for their children.

The book is divided up into six chapters:

- Chapters 1 and 2 focus on second language research and theory, respectively, whilst also considering the links between language, power and social justice.
- Chapter 3 deals with the issue of transition and discusses the impact of mobility on children's education.
- Chapter 4 raises the important issue of parental involvement.
- Chapter 5 introduces the concept of interlingual classrooms and ways of promoting the many languages of schools are outlined.
- Chapter 6 was written primarily with parents in mind, the goal being to help them choose the right school for their child. However, it is equally useful for administrators and teachers who want to review policy and practice.

As a female writer I have chosen to refer to the second language child as she and her so as to avoid the cumbersome repetition of he/she, him/her throughout the text. A detailed Glossary is provided at the end of the book.

There are many terms used for describing the second language student, I have chosen the term 'ESL student' (English as a Second Language student) as this is the term most commonly used in International Education in English-medium schools. There are several case histories throughout the text. They are illustrative rather than research evidence and have been used to introduce discussions on theory and practice.

The idea for this book came to me after I had organised the ECIS ESL & MT conference in Rome in 2005. The conference theme was *Many Languages, One Message: Equal Rights to the Curriculum* and it addressed many of the issues covered in this book. The conference was a success and it made me realise that more had to be done to make the theme a reality in all schools. As so often happens at conferences, ideas are aired and suggestions to move forward are made and then teachers go back to their respective schools and nothing happens, nothing changes.

I decided to write a book hoping that it would provoke change in schools. My initial intention was to inform parents so they could be the instigators of reform but it is parents working together with administrators and teachers that will ultimately bring about the change needed so that all children will have what they deserve: equal rights to the curriculum.

My hope is that this book will make a contribution to such reform.

Eithne Gallagher
Rome, 2008

*Chapter 1*

# Hidden and Overt Power Structures in International Schools

## Introduction

English is the medium of instruction in the vast majority of International Schools. Many of these schools have developed and grown out of what were once Overseas Schools, i.e. schools set up after the Second World War to cater for the children of businessmen from English speaking countries such as America, Canada and the United Kingdom. Many of the schools developed because of the huge resurgence of trade that brought Americans in great numbers to Europe. The curriculum used in these schools was based on various national curricula, the rationale being that children would eventually return from overseas and need to fit back into the curriculum used in their homelands.

The population of such schools is now made up largely of second language learners many of whom have never lived in America or Great Britain, nor do they plan to do so in the future. Yet many International Schools today still follow national curricula, usually American or British.

In this chapter the idea that notions and beliefs often intrinsic to national systems of education have found their way into International Education is considered. How this affects the choice of curriculum and school policies is also discussed. The main aims of this chapter are to look at:

- power structures in schools and how they may affect the ESL child;
- pedagogical choices and how they affect the second language learner;
- various programmes from the perspective of second language learners.

All of the above is discussed in the light of recent research on language acquisition.

## Research and Theory

ESL teachers in International Schools have relied on theory and research related to national systems in America, Australia, Canada and Great Britain to inform them on effective teaching and planning strategies for second language learners. However, the research in national systems (e.g. Collier & Thomas, 1997) is applicable if we bear in mind three important differences:

(1) Many International Schools are not in Anglophone countries, this means that many International School children may be exposed to the language at home (maybe more than one), English at school, plus the host country language.

(2)    Most International School children come from a relatively high socio-economic background. This suggests that these children may have access to more academic materials in the home. It is important to remember though that in the research carried out by Collier and Thomas (1997) the amount of formal schooling in the L1 (mother-tongue language) that students have received is the strongest predictor of how rapidly students will catch up in the L2 (English). This factor is a stronger predictor than socio-economic status or the extent to which the parents may or may not speak English.

(3)    Second language learners in International Schools move to a different location and encounter a new language every three years on average. In a study involving 15 International Schools, Edna Murphy found that children moved an average of 2.2 times before the age of six.

The research and theory included in the next two chapters has been produced by world authorities in the fields of language acquisition, bilingualism, applied linguistics, cognitive psychology, social linguistics and sociology. Many of the researchers mentioned have spoken at International School conferences and ESL & MT conferences. Several have visited International Schools. These researchers and theorists have been chosen because, although their research and theory is based on national systems, they know International Schools well. They have also been chosen because they are known for not staying in the ivory towers of their universities, but rather for being present in classrooms, talking with teachers and students. They have linked their research and theory to practice therefore, as Cummins says, 'they respond to issues and concerns articulated by educators' (2004: 2).

Bilingualism is cross-disciplinary, being studied in linguistics, sociology, psychology and it is also studied in relationship to power and status structures and political structures in society. Bilingualism and bilingual education cannot be understood unless connected to basic philosophies and politics in society. For more on this see Baker (2003). One of the overriding aims of International Education should be to promote *Additive Bilingualism*, that is the adding on of a second language without detracting from the maintenance or development of the first language. Cummins (2004) cites more than 150 empirical studies carried out over the past 30 years that have reported a positive association between bilingualism and students' linguistic, cognitive or academic growth.

Large scale research on second language learning is long overdue in International Education. None has been done to date.

## Politics in ESL

The decision about how to teach second language children in International Education can be very political. When a school administrator makes a statement such as, 'We are an International School not a bilingual one', this is a politically loaded affirmation. Another example is, 'English only please'. Statements such as these are not based on purely educational preferences. These speakers may have bought into the political ideal of assimilation, the process by which members of a language group lose their own language and culture, which are replaced by a different language and culture, the aim being social unity. In the USA, opponents of bilingual education support assimilation. They believe that the use of languages other than English in schools is 'unAmerican'. To these people the majority language, English, is seen as the 'fixer', the tool for unifying diversity.

International School administrators who introduce English-only policies may have taken the political stance of assimilation rather than the political idea of the rights of the individual. Teachers and administrators should be aware of how politics can affect education and be above those politics, especially when political notions hinder good practice.

Ruiz (1984) proposed three basic perspectives about language in the politics of bilingual education: language as a problem, language as a right and language as a resource. These three perspectives can also be applied to language education in International Schools.

## Language as a Problem

Schools that view language as a problem set out to 'fix' the problem. The problem is usually seen as the child's fault. They collect data on all the things the child can't do in English. Decisions may be taken to place the child in a remedial group. The child may be removed from a foreign language class until the problem with English is 'cured'. Some administrators may suggest that no use of the mother-tongue is allowed until the problem of English is resolved.

A participant at the ECIS conference in The Hague, November 2005, recounted how her administrator told the staff that she was embarrassed showing new parents around the school and hearing so much of the host country language being spoken by children in the playground. She said, 'It's putting English people off coming to our school.' This example shows that this administrator certainly viewed language as a problem. Rather than promoting the multicultural advantages of the school she was embarrassed by them.

## Language as a Right

Rather than thinking of language as a problem it is possible to consider it as a right. Many administrators and teachers who write articles for International School magazines and journals frequently quote the United Nations (UN) and the United Nations Educational, Scientific and Cultural Organisation (UNESCO) when speaking about language and international issues. The UN, UNESCO, the Council of Europe and the then European Community declared that minority language groups have the right to maintain their language. A European Community directive (25th July 1977: 77/486/EEC) pronounced that member states should promote the teaching of the mother-tongue and culture of the country of origin in the education of migrant workers' children. An international declaration such as this should not be ignored in an International School context where the majority of students have a first language that is not English. Schools that view language as a right are informed on the benefits of bilingualism and biliteracy and go out of their way to promote the learning of all their students' mother-tongues.

Baker (2003) vividly describes schools in Wales where children in the past suffered discrimination. Welsh children were banned from speaking Welsh in school. If a child was caught doing so she would be forced to wear a placard around her neck. At the end of the morning and afternoon, the last child to wear the placard would be beaten with a cane.

Discrimination such as this still exists in some International Schools. The punishment has become more subtle but the long-lasting effects remain unchanged.

Recently a Grade 1 teacher explained how she had a poster in her classroom displaying the names of all the children in her class. Every time she heard the host country language spoken by a child she would put an X next to the child's name. Young children understand very quickly that an X means wrong. Imagine the long-term effects of a small child seeing a string of X's against her name for speaking the language she knows best. The child may feel a sense of exclusion and alienation. She may even decide to stop speaking her own language. This teacher with her silencing power may be guilty of setting the process of *Subtractive Bilingualism* in motion (Subtractive Bilingualism occurs when a second language is learnt at the expense of the first language, which it gradually replaces).

Another example of language discrimination in one International School in 2006 is the practice of making Grade 2 children sit on the wall at playtime if found speaking their first language, which was in fact the host country language. Apparently the rule was imposed on teachers and students by the principal (personal communication from a primary school teacher in an International School in Italy).

Children should never be punished for speaking their own language. David Graddol at the ECIS conference in Vienna 2000 made this very clear when he said, 'it was the duty of all International School teachers to promote the learning of their students' mother-tongues'. The sad reality is that discriminative practices are still common in some International Schools. They may be carefully hidden from inspections and accreditations, but they are well known by many teachers and students.

## Language as a Resource

In a progressive International School language is viewed as a cultural and social resource for the child, for the school community and for society as a whole. Children are openly encouraged to learn through, and to think in all their languages. The languages in the classroom are many and valued equally. Teachers and students collaborate and learn from each other. Assessment procedures may reflect things children can do in English and also in their mother-tongue. There is a genuine respect for difference and a sincere attempt to develop an understanding of similarities.

Baker (2003) says that these three views, 'language as a problem', 'language as a right' and 'language as a resource', may not exist at a conscious level. They may be embedded in the subconscious assumptions of school planners and politicians. Those policy makers that see language as a problem often view the first language as a handicap to be overcome by the school. Increasing the amount of English is a way to overcome the problem but at the expense of the home language. They view developing bilingualism as an irrelevant or secondary aim of schooling.

## Relations of Power

Cummins (2001b, 2004) argues that relations of power are at the heart of schooling outcomes. When a school's relations of power are biased, ESL children's identities may not be affirmed and as a result they may remain disempowered in their schooling experience. Cummins argues that the changes in pedagogy that have taken place over the last 20 years have had little impact on the achievement levels of ESL students. The reason is that schools have failed on essential issues such as securing a very positive student identity, creating good home–school links with parents as partners in their children's education, empowering children and raising their expectations. By just teaching the given curriculum, teachers have failed to educate the whole child. This is often what the state or governing body wants – just the given curriculum. This, at its worst, is seen in the Scripted Curricula[1] used in some states in America where teachers are expected to rigorously adhere to a standard script they did not create themselves.

Some mainstream teachers in International Education have been accused of teaching only the curriculum and ignoring the Who, Where and What of the child in front of them. By this I mean:

- Who is this child?
- What makes her different from the child next to her?
- Where does she come from, not only in terms of her nationality but also her education?
- What does she carry in her cultural and linguistic baggage that I as a teacher need to know in order to instruct her fully?

These teachers are not to be blamed for their attitude. The International School that hired them may have failed to provide staff development on international mindedness, and their teacher training colleges may have failed to prepare them for working with second language learners. Many teachers do not know how to deal with children who are not monolingual. They do not understand how long it takes to learn a language or how language develops in academic contexts. They are not aware of the necessity to, 'nurture intellect and identity equally in ways that of necessity challenge coercive relations of power' (Cummins, 2004: 6).

Why are teacher training colleges not addressing these issues? Why are administrators and teachers so ill prepared to deal with second language learners? Research on Additive Bilingualism has been around a long time, as mentioned earlier. In her editorial of the *International Schools Journal* in April 2003, Edna Murphy (2003: 5–6) points out:

that of the challenges faced every day in international primary schools, there are two that stand out and neither has been properly dealt with by many of our schools. These problems cluster around the fact that many of the children speak little or no English upon their arrival at school and that at least one fifth of the students are grappling with a learning disability. Where young children are involved, and where there is an overlap between these two groups, you will find the most serious problems – serious because of the lasting consequences for children if they are not properly dealt with or, even worse, ignored. Without the right kind of help early on, the child stands little chance of academic and social success in later school years. Qualified specialists know what is best done in these areas but this alone cannot make good programmes happen; they need the support of their head.

I took this point up in my opening remarks at the ESL & MT conference in Rome in 2005. I commented:

Have you ever gone into the staff room and heard someone say, 'this child can't speak in complete sentences' or, 'that child can't write in complete sentences and how long have they been at this school?. These are common utterances in what should be very language-aware International Schools. Often the solution is, 'Well, let's cure the child, let's make her write at the sentence level until she writes well at the sentence level' or, 'This child needs more grammar lets make the ESL teacher take the child away until she's fixed before we let her loose in the content area.' We as informed ESL teachers know this is nonsense but this type of thing is common practice in too many International Schools. Why does this happen? Why are so many people good at seeing what these children *can't* do? There are too many people making decisions about ESL and MT issues who are either not informed or are misinformed. We need administrators onboard, we need the decision makers at our conferences. At the ESL Conference in Vienna 2000 we didn't have any administrators present. In Leysin ESLMT Conference in 2002 we had four. Here in Rome we have twenty and this in itself is progress!

After the Rome conference I received emails from colleagues in several International Schools telling me that their head had been present at the Rome conference and was so convinced by the arguments of the speakers that they had decided to set up a mother-tongue programme in their school. Another email told of a head of school who, on his return from the conference, called a board meeting at his school and convinced the members that they should abolish the practice of charging extra for ESL lessons.

Visionary leadership is necessary in International Education. Terry Haywood has been the head of the International School of Milan since 1985. He was chair of the board of ECIS from 1999–2001. He points out (2002: 181):

---

In contrast to the problem solving approach that is typical of pragmatic management, the visionary role for leaders in international education is better seen as that of posing questions. Such questions might include:

1. How can we provide international experience for our students?
2. How can we incorporate international themes in the curriculum?
3. How should we handle conflict resolution especially when it occurs from values that are perceived differently by different cultures?
4. What extra-curricular and student-life components are going to contribute to developing an international mindset?
5. How should issues of current affairs and global awareness be dealt with in school?
6. How can we create opportunities for international interaction where it does not occur naturally?
7. How can we forge an appreciation of the needs and aspirations of the less privileged?

It is not necessarily the role of managers to answer all of these questions but it is their role to raise these and similar concerns and to seek the involvement of the wider community (and especially the professional staff) in developing responses for the specific school context.

---

These questions could easily be inserted into accreditations and inspection documents to ascertain the international mindedness of a school. When Terry Haywood proposes that these questions should not necessarily be answered by managers but should involve the wider community and the professional staff in developing responses for their specific school context, he is, in Cummins' terms, challenging coercive relations of power (see page 9). This is indeed visionary leadership of the type found in progressive International Schools.

Let us take a closer look at Terry Haywood's first two questions: how can we provide an International Education for our students and how can we incorporate international themes in the curriculum? As soon as international teachers and administrators start conversing on these two topics and relating them both to the context of their own schools and the wider society, they will by necessity be speaking openly about all the cultures and languages in their schools. This is inclusive practice in action. These questions will open up a dialogue that will cover what the school should do about the mother-tongue languages of its students.

## Loss of Mother-Tongue: The Norm Amongst Language Minority Students

Lily Wong Fillmore's (1991) research suggests that loss or lack of continued development of the mother-tongue is the norm amongst most US language minority students. Her studies revealed that these students have difficulties communicating with their families and alienation of children from parents can occur as development progresses.

Teachers in International Schools can also affirm that this happens when the mother-tongue has not been fully developed and nurtured. Certain children may become 'wannabe' Americans or Brits to the detriment of their own language and culture and disadvantaged when they have to return to their own country.

Cummins (2004: 6) has some thought-provoking questions to ask about language loss:

- If first language loss with its problematic personal and academic consequences is extremely common among bilingual students, why is it relatively few mainstream teachers know about the issue?
- Why is it the exception rather than the rule that teachers take proactive steps to help bilingual students feel proud of their linguistic accomplishments rather than ashamed of their linguistic differences?
- Why is it still relatively uncommon for educators to encourage bilingual students to maintain and develop their home languages?

These questions need to be asked in every International School context. They have been addressed and discussed repeatedly over the years at International School conferences and in International School literature. The time has come for them to be addressed in schools.

We can also add more questions to the list, such as:

- Why are children still being discriminated against for speaking their own language in some International Schools?
- Why are administrators and teachers so under-informed about sound language acquisition practice?
- Why are children in some International Schools only given help with learning English for two years when research tells us it can take five to eight years to acquire the necessary academic skills needed to be fully operational in the curriculum?
- Why is it that some International Schools have only one or two ESL teachers when the majority of their students are second language children?
- Why do many schools not offer ongoing professional development in the areas of second language acquisition and cultural diversity?

The answers to these questions are clear. Old-fashioned International Schools do not take ESL and MT seriously. Teacher education systems have consistently ignored issues related to cultural and linguistic diversity and teachers coming from such systems are prepared only to teach monolingual children. When these teachers arrive for their first International School teaching experience, they will find the rules and curriculum have been laid down for them. The administrators and policy makers who made them were also trained to work only with monolingual children. One system reinforces and perpetuates the other.

Many teachers will follow the rules, do what they are told and carry on without questioning the rationale of teaching everyone as if their first language was English. Many first-time International School teachers and administrators may be at a loss when they find themselves dealing with multicultural children. The time these educators have to spend becoming acclimatised and learning to understand multicultural children (if they choose to do so) is time lost for the children in need.

Traditionally, policy makers are responsible for the structures in a school such as curriculum content, assessment practices and the choice of a language of instruction. If such structures act as a barrier to effective ESL instruction, then change is important. This is not an easy task as old-fashioned International Schools can be places where collaboration and innovation are not valued. There will always be enlightened teachers and administrators who are prepared to challenge the status quo and question out-dated authority that dictates poor practice, but generally such teachers and administrators move on to more effective International Schools.

In order to have an understanding of how practices such as those mentioned previously are an accepted norm in ineffective International Schools, we need to consider what Corson calls, 'Language power and social justice in education' (2001: 16).

Corson suggests that hegemony is clearly evident in the restrictive cultural environment that most schools create for children from diverse backgrounds. Cummins (2001b) sees many schools as places where children who are seen as different in some educationally relevant way are unable to negotiate their own identities. These children begin to lose their own identity before they even secure it. Remember the Grade 1 teacher mentioned earlier who marked an X next to children's names who were caught speaking their own language in her English-only classroom. As young as six years old, these children were being taught that their language is not as good as English. Cummins argues that, for education to be successful for culturally diverse students, there has to be a shift from coercive to collaborative relations of power within schools.

## Coercive Relations of Power

A *coercive relation of power* is the exercise of power by a dominant group or individual to the detriment of a dominated group or individual. In the examples cited earlier of discriminatory practice in old-fashioned International Schools, the teacher and the principal belong to the dominant group and the second language child to the dominated one.

## Collaborative Relations of Power

*Collaborative relations of power* on the other hand refer to power that can be generated in inter-group relations. Participants are empowered through collaboration; their individual identity is valued and accepted. They feel more in charge and therefore more capable of changing their lives and social situations. Power is created in the relationship and shared among participants. (An example of this is Terry Haywood's proposal that his questions be answered by involving the wider community and teachers.)

Old-fashioned International Schools often tend to follow a 'back to basics' approach to education. This implies that certain skills have to be taught and mastered (which means memorised) before adding on anything new. Many schools are presently doing a successful job of educating their children, but some are educating children to take part in a world of the past rather than preparing them for the new millennium. Often the skills in the 'back to basics' approach are dictated by a curriculum that is handed down to teachers. They may not have been involved in the writing of it, they may not approve of it, but many of them just accept it. Questioning the status quo in this type of institution may mean that you are overlooked when it comes to promotion or, worse, you may not have your contract renewed. This partly explains why many teachers remain silent in such circumstances.

Cummins (2004) suggests that teachers need to redefine their roles and the type of structures at work in schools. The interactions between educators, students and communities are never neutral. They either contribute to the disempowerment of culturally diverse students or they challenge the operation of discriminatory power structures. Old-fashioned International Schools are often intolerant of diversity at a linguistic level but able to promote it at a social level (for example the International Dress Day and the International Food Day).

Progressive International Schools on the other hand will have a curriculum in place that values all the school's languages. Cultural differences will be explored through curricular content and therefore they will become integrated into the curriculum in an authentic manner allowing children to discover their own identity and learn about the identities of others. The school community will celebrate their differences not only through food and dress but through studying world geography, world history and world religions from the perspectives of different cultures. Martin Skelton, director of the International Primary Curriculum (IPC), sums this up well (Skelton, 2002: 44):

> In the IPC we have set out with aims of helping children to discover their own national and cultural identity and to live with those whose national and cultural identities are different. If we are not careful though this apparently liberal and progressive approach will still result in division rather than union. The trick in delivering a curriculum based on this dualistic approach is the development of tolerance, empathy and mutual understanding. We are trying to encourage the development of a view that says, 'I am different and have a right to be. You are different from me with the same rights but we can live together.'

The IPC is used in more than 90 schools in 38 countries. It prides itself on addressing the issue of developing an international mindset (see http://www.internationalprimarycurriculum.com).

In progressive International Schools, sameness is not valued nor is it the ideal. Teachers and administrators collaborate with parents and the children in their care to better understand their worlds and to make their schools genuinely caring places that want to affirm every individual's identity. Children in these schools know that their voices will be heard and respected.

## Examples of Educational Structures that Reflect Coercive Relations of Power

Cummins (2004) suggests that dominant groups determine the priorities of the society and that educational institutions have historically adopted the relations of power that exist in the broader society around them. He has produced a list of examples of educational power structures that reflect coercive relations of power. These six educational structures can be found in place in many old-fashioned International Schools. The educational structures identified by Cummins that reflect coercive relations of power are:

(1)   Submersion programmes for bilingual children that actively suppress their first language, culture and identity. (Submersion is the teaching of second language students solely through the target language; in an International School context, mostly English. The child is placed in a mainstream class and left to sink or swim.)

(2)   Exclusion of culturally diverse parents from participating in their children's schooling (see Chapter 4).

(3)   Tracking or streaming that places ESL children disproportionately in lower-level tracks.

(4)   Use of biased standardised[2] tests for both achievement monitoring and special education placement.

(5)   Teacher education programmes that prepare teachers for a monolingual, monocultural, white, middle-class school population.

(6)   Curriculum content that reflects the perspectives and experiences of dominant groups and excludes those of subordinate groups.

Cummins (2004) has given clear guidelines for pointing the way forward to effective practice. International Schools accreditation bodies could turn these six statements into questions and put them into the self-evaluation documents thereby challenging old-fashioned schools into efficacy. Cummins says that educational structures such as those listed above, establish a frame that limits rather than expands the interactional space that exists between teachers and students. He also argues that societal, large scale interactions influence ways in which teachers define their roles in relation to culturally diverse students. In other words, how society feels about minority groups affects the mindset of assumptions, expectations and goals that educators bring to the task of educating students.

Here is an example given by a participant at Rome International Schools Association conference in February 2002 of societal influence and how it affected teachers at one International School:

> Recently I visited a rather prestigious International School. Upon my arrival I immediately noticed that several groups of children were walking into school with their parents and a few yards behind each family group was a man of Asian origin laden with lunch boxes, school bags and sports equipment – the donkey of the privileged. When I commented on this to teachers they said, 'Oh yes, most of our families employ people from the Philippines as maids, drivers and so on.' This International School was reinforcing the local society's view of people from the Philippines as a race of subordinated people relegated to the role of beast of burden.

Ideally International School teachers and administrators should challenge such discriminatory behaviour. However, this may prove rather difficult as many affluent parents may see nothing wrong in their actions and the immigrants may also see this as acceptable because they are happy to have found work.

Schools striving to be truly international can counter-balance this perceived relationship of master and servant through curricular content. They could conduct a world study of the movement of labour to teach children why immigrants come to wealthier countries, putting the phenomenon in a historical context to show that immigration is a common human experience that may even have involved their own ancestors.

Cummins (2004: 47) also suggests that culturally diverse students are empowered or disabled as a result of their interactions with teachers in schools. These interactions are reconciled by the role definitions (implicit or explicit) that educators take on in relation to four organisational aspects of schooling:

(1) _Language and cultural incorporation._ 'The extent to which students' language and cultural background are affirmed and promoted within the school, this includes the extent to which literacy instruction in schools affirms, builds on and extends the vernacular literacy practices that many culturally diverse students engage in outside the context of school.'
    In other words, to what extent do teachers and the curriculum promote the identity of the whole child and how do they view literacy – do they think of literacy in terms of English only or do they strive to strengthen all the child's languages by using dual language strategies?

(2) _Community/Participation._ 'The extent to which culturally diverse communities are encouraged to participate as partners in their children's

education and to contribute to the funds of knowledge that exist in their communities to this educational partnership (Moll *et al.*, 1992).'

In other words, what measures does the school take to actively involve ESL parents in the life of the school? And what do teachers do to encourage parents to become involved in their children's education? Do they explicitly invite them to bring their personal and cultural knowledge to the classroom and the school?

(3) *Pedagogy*. 'The extent to which instruction promotes intrinsic motivation on the part of students to use language actively in order to generate their own knowledge, create literature and art and act on social realities that affect their lives. The alternative to what Freire (1983) termed a banking education where the teacher defines her role as depositing information in the students' memory banks.' (An example of this is the 'back to basics' approach mentioned earlier where the teachers teach a skill until the child has mastered it, i.e. stored it in her memory bank.)

In other words, how does the teacher organise instruction so that the child is motivated to use language in an active way, to be creative and also to think about her life and make choices that affect it? Does the teacher involve the child in critical thinking rather than giving the child knowledge to learn and regurgitate?

(4) *Assessment*. 'The extent to which professionals involved in assessment become advocates for students by focusing primarily on the ways in which students' academic difficulty is a function of interactions within the school context rather than legitimising the location of the "problem" within the students.'

In other words, how do teachers assess students? Do they focus on all the things the child can't do or are they able to see all the things the child can do? Do they see the things the child can't do as the child's problem or are they open-minded enough to see limitations in the school's structure that may impede the child's learning?

It is the negotiation of identity between teachers and students that is central to students' academic success or failure. Students need to be able to relate the curriculum to their own experience and learn to analyse broader social issues that are relevant to their lives. Teachers should have a clear identity of who they are as educators – know what they believe in, know what works in the classroom and why. Teachers should also be aware of the identity options they offer to their students, i.e. do they train them to sit quietly and passively absorb information or do they encourage them to think critically and collaboratively and take action? Teachers should also have an image of the society their students will take part in.

Pedagogical approaches differ in International Schools. Many follow Traditional Pedagogy some Progressive Pedagogy and others use Critical Inquiry as a transformative approach to pedagogy. We will now take a look at these three approaches and identify why the Transformative Pedagogy/Critical Inquiry approach has most relevance for international educators.

## Traditional Pedagogy

In *Traditional Pedagogy* the teacher's main job is to pass on knowledge and skills to the student. The teacher starts and controls the interactions in the classroom, guiding them towards the instructional objectives. Class work is often based on workbook exercises and structured drills. The teaching of language is divided up into skills for example, phonics, vocabulary and grammar rules. These are often taught in isolation from each other. All learning is believed to happen in a hierarchical order starting with more simple elements and gradually moving on to more complex forms. Knowledge is something to be learnt and reproduced when the teacher or the system requires it.

In the classroom-based research carried out by Ramirez *et al.* (1991) they observed that in over half the interactions that teachers had with students, the students did not produce any language as most of the time they listened or responded with non-verbal gestures or actions e.g. 'Raise your hand if . . . '. When students did respond, it was simply to tell the teacher back what she had just said. The teachers offered a passive learning environment that limited the students' opportunities to produce language and also to develop more complex language and thinking skills. Traditional Pedagogy is a form of banking or empty vessel education. A common question pattern in a Traditional Pedagogy classroom is a teacher asks a question she knows the answer to, and the child responds often with a single word answer, and then the teacher replies assessing the answer – filling up the 'bank' or vessel. This is sometimes referred to as the transmission model of education.

## Progressive Pedagogy

*Progressive Pedagogy* is based on the work of Dewey, Montessori and Piaget. The founding principles of Progressive Pedagogy are that students are active learners, they learn by doing and that education is not simply a matter of receiving information but rather a means of intelligent inquiry and thought. The child is placed at the centre of the educational process. Progressive Pedagogy in schools is often referred to as Child Centred Learning. The process of learning is more important than the content. Learning should be meaningful to the child rather than something to memorise for test purposes. Effective learning is relevant to the individual rather than being imposed by an institution. Traditional approaches to language teaching break the language up into parts so it is easier to transmit. Progressive approaches often insist that language can be learnt only when it is kept whole and used for meaningful communication.

In Progressive Pedagogy knowledge is viewed as a catalyst for further inquiry in contrast to Traditional Pedagogy where it is seen as what you can remember of what you have been taught. In progressive classrooms the construction of meaning is important as is inquiry through collaboration. The classroom is a community of learners where knowledge is produced through students and teachers working together. The focus remains on the child within the learning community. Tolerance and acceptance are often passively suggested through exhibitions aimed at celebrating diversity but students are not encouraged to reflect on their own experience critically or to study social realities from a critical perspective.

Traditional Pedagogy models tend to work against one of the central principles of language learning: that using the language in interactions with others is the way language is learned (Swain, 1995). Traditional approaches also tend to present a curriculum that means something only to the dominant culture and so ESL students find it difficult to express their own experiences and views when these are different from those held by the broader society. Many traditional approaches to ESL focus on the drilling of low-level skills perpetuating the second language students' difficulties with the curriculum by keeping them trapped in situations where discourse is minimal and meaningless. This type of banking education devalues the identities of ESL students. Their prior knowledge remains untapped. They are not given opportunities to think critically about social realities that affect their own life. Students are often silenced or made 'voiceless' in the classroom (Giroux, 1991). According to Cummins (2004), they are being prepared to accept the societal status quo and their own inferior status within it.

The instructional beliefs inherent in Progressive Pedagogy are supported by research. Social assumptions and social realities, however, are not addressed. The focus is on the child and on her learning environment. Teachers encourage students to think about their experiences and stimulate the development of their self-esteem. However, Progressive Pedagogy often avoids the broader social realities of life beyond the classroom. ESL students need to understand and be able to articulate the language that will allow them to participate fully in the dominant society. In order to do this students need to be able to analyse what is going on in the world and be able to relate it to themselves.

## Transformative Pedagogy (Critical Inquiry)

Cummins (2004) makes the provocative statement, 'Transformative Pedagogy: Who needs it?' Progressive International Education needs *Transformative Pedagogy*, but first let us take a look at what exactly it means.

Transformative Pedagogy uses Critical Inquiry to enable students to analyse and understand the social realities of their own lives and of their communities. Students discuss, and frequently act in ways in which these realities might be transformed through various forms of social action. Instruction aims, Cummins says, 'to go beyond the sanitised curriculum that is still the norm in most schools. It strives to develop a *Critical Literacy*' (2004: 260).

Transformative Pedagogy's main concern is social injustice and how to transform undemocratic or oppressive institutions. It helps provide students with the necessary implements to better themselves and strives to create a more just society. Cummins suggests that teachers and students need to develop an understanding of the interdependence between ideology, power and culture so they can rise to the challenge of transforming any undemocratic social or institutional practices that support inequalities and oppressive social identities and realities. Giroux (1994: 30) states that 'Pedagogy in the critical sense illuminates the relationship among knowledge, authority and power'. Freire (Freire & Macedo, 1987) tells us that our students must learn to read not only the word but also the world.

Teachers who follow Transformative Pedagogical models know that culture, language, history, power and politics condition and form how social realities are understood and defined inside and outside classrooms. Often educational decisions are based on ideologies that are not grounded in educational theory but rather on beliefs influenced by politics, history, language, culture and more importantly power. Teachers need to question what they teach, why they teach it and how effective the teaching–learning process is.

As indicated earlier in this chapter, many teachers arrive in International Schools ill prepared to do the job. When they find themselves in establishments that follow a traditional type of pedagogy that excludes ESL learners, some teachers carry on regardless. They do not question the ethos of ignoring the child in the classroom who doesn't speak English. This is one of the reasons that International Education needs Transformative Pedagogy. International training schemes need to address the issue of power relations within and outside the classroom. Large scale training for International School teachers is necessary for change to occur in our schools.

Biliteracy should be one of the main components of international educational reform. However, this in itself is insufficient. Education objectives should incorporate literacy, cultural and Critical Literacy goals if students are to learn to 'read the world' as well as to 'read the word' (Freire & Macedo, 1987).

According to Corson (2001), throughout most of the history of schooling in English speaking countries, ESL children have not had the valuable start that bilingual education offers. Whole communities have been made to feel ashamed of their first language. This latter point was illustrated earlier: the tendency to make children ashamed of speaking their first language at the young age of six is thriving in some schools that call themselves international.

## The International Baccalaureate Organisation: Creates Programmes that Would Teach Children to Have Open Minds.

The origins of the International Baccalaureate Organisation (IBO), or rather the rationale behind it, grew out of a meeting called by UNESCO in 1949. This is the first known official inter-continental meeting of schools coming together with a common cause. Their aim was to further international understanding and world peace through education. This was followed in the summer of 1950 by a course for teachers interested in International Education organised by the Council of International Schools (CIS) at the International School of Geneva. (The International School of Geneva is known as the birthplace of the IBO and even today, to its credit, it is still at the forefront of International Education.)

The 50 teachers and administrators who attended that first course came from schools in Asia, Europe and the United States. They came up with this first known definition of International Education:

It should give the child an understanding of his past as a common heritage to which all men irrespective of nation, race or creed have contributed and which all men should share; it should give him an understanding of his present world as a world in which peoples are interdependent and in which cooperation is a necessity.

In such an education emphasis should be laid on a basic attitude of respect for all human beings as persons, understanding of those things which unite us and an appreciation of the positive values of those things which may seem to divide us, with the objective of thinking free from fear or prejudice.

(Course for Teachers Interested in International Education, 1950. (Hill, 2002: 22))

From these early beginnings the IBO was established in 1968. It is a non-profit, international educational foundation registered in Switzerland. The IBO offers a series of International Education programmes for children from 3 to 19 (or more) years of age. These programmes are used by more than 1800 schools in over 100 countries (2006 data). More on the programmes offered by the IBO is given later in this chapter.

This section focuses on the pedagogical beliefs that led to the IBO's creation and how it challenged traditional practices by, amongst other things, introducing Critical Inquiry into its programmes and by promoting the notion of 'world citizenship' through which students learn attitudes that encourage positive action for a better world.

We will also consider whether it is possible to measure the ideological dimension of International Education, as promoted by the IBO, through school accreditations, through administrator and teacher accountability and through student performance.

In his article, 'The History of International Education: An International Baccalaureate Perspective', Ian Hill (2002) tells us that the IB Diploma came into being because there was a need for an internationally recognised diploma that would act as an international passport to International Education and assist global mobility. The important pragmatic elements contained in the course were learning about other cultures and world issues and being able to speak other languages. Hill says that is was clear to the teachers involved in setting up this ground-breaking course that a new pedagogical approach was needed – an approach that would promote international understanding and do away with stereotypes and prejudices. In his words (Hill, 2002: 19):

Critical inquiry coupled with an open mind, willing to question established beliefs, willing to withdraw from conventional positions in the light of new evidence and experiences, willing to accept that being different does not mean being wrong. This was quite a change from the emphasis at the time on accumulating knowledge as fact by memorisation.

The IBO was born out of ideological, utilitarian and pedagogical considerations. Its goals were:

- to provide a perspective that would promote international understanding, prepare students for world citizenship and promote peace;
- to provide a school-leaving diploma that would be recognised for university entrance around the world with common curriculum and examinations and;
- to promote critical thinking skills (rather than an emphasis on encyclopaedic knowledge) via a balanced programme in the humanities, the experimental sciences and experiential learning (Hill, 2002: 20).

Hill then goes on to point out that the most important skill to develop in students is the ability to analyse critically the information that has been presented to them. He defines areas of knowledge such as:

- understanding why cultural behaviour is different;
- understanding how nations are and to what extent they are interdependent;
- understanding which areas of sustainable development need most attention;
- understanding how language is related to culture in a very complex manner;
- understanding what are the elements of peace and of conflict.

Hill asks, how can knowledge such as current events be understood and analysed in terms of these areas of knowledge? He argues this requires a pedagogical approach that places importance on critical thinking skills, working collaboratively, independent research, interdisciplinarity, developing the 'whole person' and learning how to learn. Hill suggests (2002: 27) that '[a]ttitudes are the effective part of the whole person' and on the basis of this goes on to propose the following definition of the ideology in International Education:

- commitment to social justice on a world scale;
- empathy for the feelings, needs and lives of others in different countries;
- respect for cultural diversity within and without one's geographical location;
- a belief that people can make a difference;
- concern for the environment on a global scale;
- commitment to sustainable development on a global scale.

At its conception, the IBO appeared to point out the limitations of Traditional Pedagogy and sought to introduce Critical Inquiry into curricular content. This can be seen in the following excerpt from IBO's mission statement (IBO, 1996):

> Strong emphasis is placed on the ideals of international understanding and responsible citizenship, to the end that IB students may become critical and compassionate thinkers, lifelong learners and informed participants in local and world affairs, conscious of the shared humanity that binds all people together while respecting the variety of cultures and attitudes that makes for the richness of life.

In his conclusion, however, Hill points out that the skills that the IBO seeks to develop in its three programmes: the Primary Years Programme (PYP), the Middle Years Programme (MYP) and the Diploma Programme (IBD), can only be measured through the actions of individuals during their lifetime. He says this concept of ongoing 'world citizenship' is fundamental to International Education and that it comprises three levels:

(1)  the practical level of learning knowledge about content;
(2)  the pedagogical level of understanding and applying the content to events through critical analysis;
(3)  having attitudes that lead to positive action for a better world.

Hill believes that points one and two above are easily measured and lead to students being informed participants in local and world affairs. However, he adds a note of caution using the words of Hayden who, in a paper presented to the IBO advisory committee in 2001, said that students can attain points one and two without ever achieving point three. Hayden (2001: 28 )says: 'The pragmatic dimensions may be developed without the ideological dimension necessarily being nurtured.' She argues:

> [It is] only when students are compassionate thinkers, conscious of the shared humanity that binds people together and respecting the variety of cultures and attitudes that makes for the richness of life, will the possibility of establishing an ideology in international education exist. And this, the most important objective, can only be measured through the actions of individuals during their lifetime.

If we accept that 'Internationalism is a duty of all genuine education' (Orellano Benado, 1998: 12), then it is time to establish an ideology of Internationalism in International Education that can be measured through the accreditation process, through administrator and teacher accountability and through student performance. Administrators, teachers and students can be measured through their actions in school:

- Do teachers and administrators buy into the concept of international mindedness?
- How is this evident in the way decisions are made in the school, in curriculum content and in the way the curriculum is delivered and assessed?
- What actions do administrators, teachers and students take to tackle the social realities of our times and relate them to their own lives?

Michael Allan is the Intercultural Awareness Leader at the International School of Amsterdam in the Netherlands. He is a member of the ECIS Cross Culture Committee. Mike has developed a flexible tool 'the Internationalism Audit' for measuring Internationalism in schools. He describes it here in his own words:

**An Internationalism Audit**
*Michael Allan*

Although international understanding or intercultural awareness forms part of the declared philosophy of IBO and other international schools, very few would be able to point to a coherent, monitored and evaluated programme for internationalism. The difficulty lies in developing an instrument for evaluation which is valid across cultures and applicable in widely differing school situations. A quality assurance programme for internationalism must look to other than traditional process and structural factors in order to evaluate and improve effectiveness in this respect. The essence and medium of intercultural learning lie in differences, and the cultural dissonance they produce permeates all aspects of the school culture. In a case study of intercultural learning in an international school (Allan, 2003), it was found that intercultural awareness was determined in the domains of peer support, teacher support, own language and culture teaching, ESL teaching, induction programmes, social and extra-curricular activities, inter-cultural training in the curriculum and in-service teacher training.

Performance indicators for these domains were developed over several years at a series of teachers' workshops around the world, where international teachers were asked to give concrete examples of what they would expect to see in a school that was effective in these areas of international understanding. These compiled give a flexible instrument, an Internationalism Audit, for assessing school effectiveness in the area of international understanding, which is emic in nature and can be individually tailored for any school.

Adapted from Allan (2003)

An example of Allan's Internationalism Audit is given in Appendix 1.

The declared aim of all IB programmes is, 'to develop internationally minded people who, recognizing their common humanity and shared guardianship of the planet, help to create a better and more peaceful world' (IBO, 2006: 5). How wonderful it would be if this could be an aim of all schooling everywhere.

Schools need to investigate how fully international they are. Allan's Internationalism Audit could become a component of accreditations or school self-appraisals. It pinpoints key areas such as mother-tongue language teaching, effective ESL programme, cultural affirmation and intercultural learning in the curriculum, to name but a few. These areas can be measured and the information gained used to highlight both strengths and weaknesses in judging how truly international a school is.

Critical Literacy can be an effective means of implementing what the IBO proposes: developing internationally minded children who are 'compassionate thinkers', able to assert their rights to equality of opportunity and power.

## Critical Literacy

Critical Literacy challenges the status quo. It involves questioning received knowledge and makes clear the connection between knowledge and power. Students need to learn how to read the *world* and not only the *word* (Freire & Macedo, 1987). When teachers introduce Critical Literacy into the curriculum, by inviting students to develop critical thought and action on various subject matters, the teacher becomes more informed of the child's identity and needs. The teacher and child become involved in a more genuine mutual learning process where each one learns from the other. If we want children to leave our schools prepared to take action in order to 'create a better and more peaceful world', we need to make them think and put their thoughts into action.

Old-fashioned International Schools tend to believe that Critical Literacy is suitable only for older students.

Alma Flor Ada (1988a, 1988b) proposes a framework for Critical Literacy, an approach to literacy education based on the work of Paulo Freire. The approach is applicable to students at any grade level. It is divided up into four phases in what she terms, 'the creative act of reading'. Each phase involves an interactional process between either the teacher and students or, between the students and their peers. This interactional process progressively opens up meaningful articulation and the amplification of students' voices. The reading texts used in this approach come from current events, newspapers or mainstream content areas. Ada emphasises that although the phases are discussed separately, 'In a creative reading act they may happen concurrently and be interwoven' (1988b: 103). Cummins illustrates these phases in Figure 1.

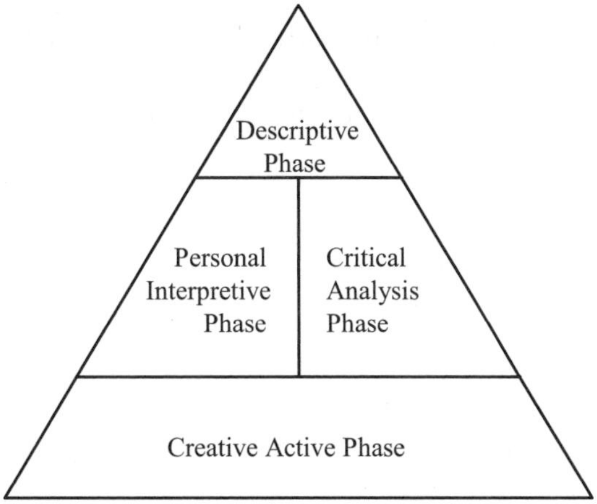

**Figure 1** The creative act of reading
*Source*: Cummins (2001a: 274)

## Descriptive phase

In the Descriptive Phase the main focus of interaction is on the information contained in the text. The kind of questions asked at this level might be: Where? When? How did it happen? Who did it? and Why? These are typical reading comprehension questions for which it is easy to find the answers in the text itself. Ada suggests, however, that reading that stays at this level is passive and receptive. When instruction remains at this level it maintains a safe distance from any challenge to society's power structure. This phase focuses on basic literacy skills isolated from cultural and Critical Literacy.

## Personal interpretive phase

After the information in the text has been discussed, students relate it to their own experience and feelings. The questions the teacher might ask in the Personal Interpretive Phase are: Have you ever seen/felt/experienced anything like that? How did you feel? Did you like it? Did it make you happy? Did it frighten you? What about your family?

Ada says these kinds of questions help develop the children's self-esteem because they show the child that her experiences are valued by the teacher and her peers. This process also helps children to understand that 'true learning occurs only when the information received is analysed in the light of one's own experiences and emotions' (Ada, 1988a: 104). There has to be an atmosphere of trust and acceptance in the classroom and this is very necessary if students and teachers are to risk sharing their emotions and experiences. This sharing and reflecting opens up the classroom to recognising personal and cultural identities. This does not tend to happen in Traditional Pedagogy where the interpretation of text is not discussed on a personal level and thus a mirror image of the dominant group's notion of cultural literacy is maintained. The Personal Interpretive Phase deepens students' comprehension of the text and issues being discussed by placing the knowledge firmly in the students' own histories. It also develops real cultural literacy in that it integrates students' own experiences with content from the mainstream curriculum.

## Critical analysis phase

Once children have compared and contrasted what is presented in the text with their own experiences, they move onto the abstract process of critically analysing the issues or problems raised in the text. This leads to them making deductions and exploring what generalisations can be made. The teacher's questions in this phase might include: Is it valid? When is it valid? Does it benefit everyone in the same way? Are there any alternatives to this situation? Would people of different cultures, classes or genders have behaved differently? How? Why? Ada points out that school children of all ages can engage in this type of critical process; however their analysis will obviously reflect their experiences and level of maturity. This phase extends children's comprehension of the text by actively encouraging them to examine the coherence of the information and evaluate it against their knowledge and perspectives.

Cummins (2001a) suggests that when children pursue guided research and critical reflection, they are not only involved in a process of knowledge generation, they are also involved in the process of defining who they are as individuals. Through issues that affect their lives, students gain the power to resist external definitions of who they are.

## Creative action phase

This is a phase of turning the results of the previous phases into real or concrete action. The interaction is guided towards discovering what changes individuals can make to improve their lives or resolve the problem or issue that has been presented. Imagine for example that students have been studying problems related to environmental pollution. They have read local newspaper articles or researched periodicals such as *National Geographic* and Greenpeace magazines to find examples of problems related to environmental pollution. They have related these issues to their own experiences, critically analysed the causes and possible solutions. Now, in this action phase, students might decide to write to a politician or write an article for the school magazine highlighting the issue to sensitise other students. They might write a letter to a local newspaper outlining the problem or start a petition in the area to nudge the local authorities into action. They could write a play that analyses the issue. This phase can be seen as extending comprehension to the point where students and teachers collaborate to transform aspects of their social realities and, as Cummins says, by doing so they gain a deeper understanding of those realities.

Ada's framework demonstrates that comprehension can take place at different levels. If we stop at level one, we remain at the level of functional literacy and this is the reality of children learning according to a back to basics approach in some International School contexts. When the process is stopped at level one, the knowledge remains static rather than becoming a catalyst for further exploration and ultimately action. The more students progress through the pyramid in Figure 1, the more they develop their understanding. The Personal Interpretive Phase deepens the individual student's comprehension by placing the knowledge directly into the personal and cultural experiences that make up their individual stories. The process is also helped by the sharing of this information through collaboration with teachers and peers. The cultural analysis phase extends comprehension further by encouraging students to juxtapose the internal logical coherence of the information in the text, with other knowledge and perspectives they already have. Finally the Creative Action Phase represents concrete, real action that aims to transform aspects of their social realities and helps to deepen their understanding of the issues.

Ada's framework is an example of Transformative Pedagogy in action. Transformative Pedagogy can help establish ideology in international education: an ideology that lends itself to being measured both in terms of the quality of its application (measured by accrediting organisations) and in the level of student results obtained (measured by the school itself).

Awareness of the social realities of our times and the need to question and analyse the societal power relations from multiple perspectives needs to be built into international curricula from the age of four onwards. The younger children are when they start using knowledge to elaborate their own decisions and actions, the more practice they get in doing so throughout their schooling and the more likely the chances are they will continue to do so throughout their lifetimes. ESL children need pedagogy that recognises, appreciates and develops their identity.

## Socio-Cultural and Socio-Historical Learning Theories

In Transformative Pedagogy educators encourage the development of the student's voice through critical reflection on their experience and social issues. Language and meaning are seen as being inseparable and knowledge becomes a catalyst for further action. This view is in agreement with the Vygotskian view of learning which may be considered another example of Transformative Pedagogy in action.

Lev Vygotsky was a Russian psychologist who lived at the beginning of the 20th century. His work however was not widely translated until the 1960s. Since the 1980s his work has been a major influence on educational theory in Western Europe, North America and Australia. His theory broadly termed socio-cultural or socio-historical offers a different perspective to what is traditionally given by dominant Western psychological theories but has much in common with Cummins' arguments in favour of Transformative Pedagogy.

Vygotsky (1978) outlined the ways that teachers can intervene and arrange effective learning by challenging and extending the child's current state of development. He called this the *Zone of Proximal Development* (ZPD). By this he meant the cognitive gap between what a child can do unaided and what the child could do working with a more skilled expert (peers or teachers). The ZPD is the interpersonal space where minds meet and new understandings are formed through collaborative interaction and Critical Inquiry. The child initially participates in joint thinking but eventually the external social dialogue is internalised to become an important resource for individual thinking. He refers to this as 'inner speech'. The objective of learning is not to learn items of knowledge but to learn how to use knowledge in different contexts.

We want children to learn to think rather than us telling them what to think. The transformative approach fits in well with the ideology inherent in the IB programmes. If we are to prepare all our students to become the IBO's, 'critical and compassionate thinkers', we need to start well before the child is in senior education. The IBO has made this its business in recent years by introducing the PYP and MYP.

## The Evolution of the IBO

Since the IBO's origins in 1950, some six decades have passed. The IBO now offers three programmes that give much needed continuity from kindergarten right through to the final year of schooling. These programmes are PYP, the MYP and the IBD. Innovative and committed teachers from many different cultures have played an important role in the creation of these programmes. The IBO has a research unit at the University of Bath in the UK where they offer research projects and degrees in International Education, and many teachers and administrators from International Schools are involved in these.

International Education is indebted to the contribution the IBO has made. When choosing an International School, parents are often advised to choose one that follows IB programmes rather that one that uses national or in-school developed curricula. The reason is simple: money has been invested into researching these programmes and enlightened teachers and administrators have been involved in their creation. The IBO has now recognised the importance of Additive Bilingualism and consequently the importance of mother-tongue development (in its curriculum standards, listed amongst common practices, is the following: 'The school actively supports the development of the mother-tongue language of all students.'). Much of the credit for this must go to the ECIS ESL & MT Committee. This committee is made up of teachers from International Schools who are interested in the advancement of second language and mother-tongue languages in International Schools. In 2000 the ESL Committee, as it was then known, held a conference in Vienna. There was intense discussion on the importance of developing students' mother-tongue led by David Graddol. At the end of the conference, there was overwhelming agreement that more had to be done on this issue in International Education.

Teachers decided to petition ECIS asking to change the committee name to the ESL *and Mother-Tongue* Committee in order to raise awareness on this issue and also to stress that the two, English language and mother-tongue language, go hand in hand.

The first ever ECIS ESL & MT conference was held in Leysin in 2002. The committee invited Virginia Collier and Wayne Thomas to present their monumental research project which came to the fundamental conclusion that:

> Of all the student background variables, the most powerful predictor of academic success in L2 [English] is formal schooling in L1 [mother-tongue].
> (Collier & Thomas, 1997: 39)

Because of these conferences International Schools have taken small steps forward. CIS accreditation documents now ask what schools do to promote the learning of mother-tongue languages. More International Schools have mother-tongue programmes and, importantly, the three IB programmes now make a conscious effort to further mother-tongue learning.

## The IB Primary Years Programme

The IB PYP is in the process of developing a guide for second language learners. Schools that offer PYP have to train their teachers and administrators in the use of the programme. This can be done through school-based training, organised by the IBO, or by attending IBO workshops. At the core of the PYP philosophy is the belief that PYP teachers are concerned with:

> The total growth of the developing child touching hearts as well as minds.
>
> (IBO, 2002a: 1)

## The IB Middle Years Programme

The IB MYP has high quality printed guidelines for effective ESL and mother-tongue provision. Below is an excerpt from the IBO's *Second-language acquisition and mother-tongue development: a guide for schools* (IBO, 2004: 12):

> Maintaining and developing language and literacy skills in the mother-tongue:
>
> - Ensures cognitive development
> - Enables students to remain in touch with, and maintain esteem for, the language, literature and culture of their home country
> - Leads to Additive Bilingualism
> - Has the potential to increase intercultural awareness and understanding both for the students and their peers
> - Makes it possible for students to readjust to life in their home community and educational system should they return to their home country

## The IB Diploma Programme

The IBD Programme has Language A1, which is a two-year course of study in the literature of the student's mother-tongue or best language. In the schools guide to the diploma programme it states:

> Provided there is sufficient and written literature in a language and the request is received well in advance of the examinations, Language A1 examinations are provided in any language no matter how rarely or widely spoken it may be. Therefore beyond the 45 languages readily available the IBO offer a wide range from Albanian, Asante and Bemba to Xhosa, Yoruba and Zulu.
>
> (IBO, 2002b: 8)

Allowing students to study their own language in this way means the IBO has made a commitment to mother-tongue languages of children in International Education, giving them the option of taking an exam in their mother-tongue in their final year of schooling. The IBD Programme stipulates that the Extended Essay (a compulsory 4000-word essay submitted by all IBD candidates) can be also written in the student's own language.

The IBD also offers a Language A2 course which is the study of the language and literature of the student's second language. It is designed for students with a high level of competence in the target language, which is often English for ESL students. Its main focus is the reinforcement and refinement of language skills.

## Is just providing an IBO programme enough to promote change?

The IBO has become increasingly more concerned with addressing the issues of ESL and mother-tongue in its programmes. However, a word of warning is necessary here. Schools can stray from the principles and beliefs of the IBO without anyone being aware. A school, for example, may tell you that your child cannot take the IB Diploma because her maths skills are weak. This is just not true. The IB offers most courses at one of two levels, standard or higher (in mathematics there are even three levels) and a student who is less able in a subject should be directed towards the subject's standard level course. In fact the IBO does not recommend pre-course selection.

A colleague, a retired administrator, had this problem:

His son was attending an International School that followed the IB at diploma level. When the child was 15 his father was called into school and told that, because of his son's low grades and especially because of his weakness with maths, he would not be able to do the IB Diploma. Luckily for the child his father was a well-informed educator, he knew his child was a happy go lucky 15 year old, not terribly interested in school at that particular period, but he also knew his son was a capable boy. More to the point, his father was aware that there was no selection process for the IB Diploma. He promptly withdrew his child from the school and enrolled him in another International School. The child passed the IB with 34 points (the passing grade is 24), obtaining a 4 out of 7 in maths.

Imagine what could have happened to this child had his father not taken action. The teacher and the school had told the child he was a failure and not capable of taking the IB. This school did not seriously believe in instilling a lifelong love of learning nor did it show any understanding of the 'whole' child.

This is just one example of an International School that advertises itself as an IB school but obviously does not embrace the fundamental principles that the IBO promotes.

A further example regards a core part of the IBD Programme, the compulsory Creative Action Service (CAS). To complete the CAS part of their programme, students are expected to dedicate three to four hours a week, over the two-year course, to creative and social activities. However . . .

Once when I was giving a workshop I shared how I had used an IB student who spoke Arabic to help a new arrival with understanding key concepts in social studies. I explained how the student worked with the child a couple of periods a week clocking up the time for the Social Action Services component of her IB Diploma. It was a very successful experience for both students. A participant in the workshop raised her hand and said, 'In my school children invent their CAS hours. They have so much studying to do they don't have the time for that as well.'

This teacher's school did not take one of the core components of the IB Diploma seriously. They adopted a simple box-ticking mentality: the student says she has completed a certain number of hours and a tick is placed in a box without question. This school did not teach the child the importance of acting on social realities nor did it instil concern for others and so on that IB seeks to promote.

Effective International Schools explain the rationale behind CAS to parents and students alike. They ensure that students have really completed their CAS hours before issuing them with a diploma. Parents have an important role to play here too. They need to be involved and help their child understand the importance of having a strong sense of civic responsibility and being involved in both their local and the wider community.

Here is an example of CAS hours successfully implemented:

When my son was studying for his IB and was trying to come up with what he could do for CAS hours, my husband suggested he went to a local old peoples' home to enquire if they needed help. There he met a man in his 50s who was in the home because he had been blind from birth and his family could no longer take care of him. It was arranged that my son would take Umberto out for walks on Sunday mornings. When my son finished his CAS hours he continued taking Umberto for walks, when the weather was bad Umberto came to our house and regaled us with Neapolitan recipes he had learnt from his mother as a young boy and would sing beautiful Neapolitan songs.

When our son went away to university my husband kept up the Sunday morning tradition until Umberto was eventually moved to an old peoples' home in another area. The IBO CAS hours helped us a family do something in the local community that we may not have otherwise thought of. It opened our eyes to the plight of people living in institutions and it brought a brief respite to a man immobilised because he couldn't see.

Another example of schools not fully embracing the IBO's underlying beliefs regards the placing of students in the various language courses available. Sometimes students are placed in one of the courses designed for second language students where the language being studied is in fact their own language, thus ensuring a high grade.

It might be thought that teachers would be able to address these wrongdoings through the accreditation process when schools do their self-evaluation study. Again this depends on the integrity of the administration. In some schools teachers are deliberately left out of the process for fear of what they will say. In some instances, the visiting inspectors do not take what teachers say seriously enough. Here is an example of this from an ESL colleague:

> As chair of the Language Arts Committee in our school I wrote down the perceived reasons for change and why we needed a second ESL teacher and so on. I pointed out clearly that the school did not meet the standards written in the accreditation document in many areas. My hope was that the inspectors would see clearly that things needed to change. Instead they told us that we were being too hard on ourselves and that really we were meeting the standards better that we realised.

One can see clearly that challenging the hidden power structures in International Education is not easy.

None of the things mentioned previously should take place in an International School but they do. A lot depends on the integrity of the school. A major strength of the accreditation process is the fact that its very existence obliges schools to perform self-evaluation. There are, however, weaknesses in the process. Without doubt there are many successful and thorough team visits but effectiveness depends on who is in the visiting team and how experienced they are at evaluating. Not always does the visiting team get a true picture of what goes on in a school.

Schools straying from IB principles and beliefs are likely to be ineffective schools that do not value staff development and that are run purely as a business. The IB may be offered at the higher level only, perhaps simply to be competitive with other schools in the area rather than because of any real belief in, or understanding of, its basic philosophy. These schools take neither the IBO's values nor its standards seriously.

There are, however, plenty of schools that do justice to the IB and some that are so convinced of the rationale that they have invested in all three of its programmes.

## Some statistics

The International School Consultancy (ISC) has a data-sharing and cooperation agreement with the CIS. In October 2006 its website (http://www.iscresearch.com) stated that there were 4104 International Schools in 186 countries. Of these, 3548 were English-medium schools. According to ISC, over 250 new schools were added to their database in the year ending August 2006 alone, suggesting a growth rate of over 6%. At this rate the total number of International Schools will be well over 5000 by the year 2012.

The IBO website's statistics page (http://www.ibo.org/facts/schoolstats) shows the total number of schools offering one or more IBO programmes in 2006 was 1875 in 124 countries but of this number only 87 schools were offering all three programmes. Figure 2 provides a complete picture of the use of IBO programmes in International Schools in 2006.

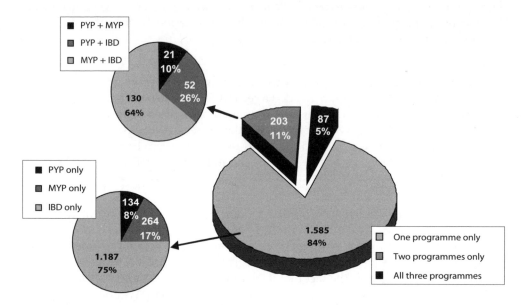

**Figure 2**   Use of IBO Programmes in 2006
*Source*: Data from http://www.ibo.org/facts/schoolstats

Given the difference between the total number of International Schools and the number of those that offer at least one IBO programme, it appears obvious that many schools are following national or state curricula or some other programme. Why? Perhaps because they cannot pay for further training for teachers, maybe they feel the IBO curriculum might be too restrictive. Whatever the reasons, they make the job of choosing the right school for your child difficult.

## A valid alternative

The International School of Brussels (ISB) is a progressive International School that opted out of published programmes, considering them overly fragmented, complex, bureaucratic and too expensive to satisfy the requirements of true Internationalism. ISB is a CIS/MSA (Middle States Association) accredited school that offers the IB at diploma level only and even in the higher grades is developing valid alternatives to the IB Diploma. At all grade levels, the school's goal is to engage students with: 'What kids really need to learn, like the global issues that threaten the future of humankind' (personal communication from K. Bartlett, Aug. 2006). In developing their curriculum they have focused on school-wide themes that explore human commonalities from the multiple perspectives of a diverse student population.

Kevin Bartlett, director of ISB, outlines below the ISB model of an international curriculum in this way:

---

The International School of Brussels has developed an alternative model of international curriculum that provides a comprehensive and coherent programme of learning, from Nursery to Grade 12. In so doing it has addressed the weaknesses perceived by the school in current published models, as follows:

### Central Assessable Mission

The school is driven by clear values: Everyone included, everyone challenged, everyone successful. It works hard to live up to this, ensuring that, for example, no child is excluded from a 'diploma' for reasons of learning disability.

### Common Outcomes

The school's mission also commits ISB to developing International Citizens and Independent Learners. Critically, these are defined using the facets of understanding developed by Grant Wiggins and Jay McTighe, in the Understanding by Design programme, as follows:

Independent Learner = intellectual understanding = explain, interpret, apply.
International Citizen = human understanding = empathy, perspective, self-knowledge.

### Clear Standards

Equally critically, these facets of understanding and their attendant vocabulary have been used to develop a continuum of broad, understanding-based standards, N-12, in all learning areas or 'literacies'. This places the school in the rare position of, literally, being able to assess its mission. It also completes and complements a commitment to learning through inquiry. The ISB curriculum views inquiry as a valuable process, understanding as an invaluable product.

### Continuity through Character

The school's standards in themselves provide continuity. They also incorporate a set of dispositional standards, aspects of character to which the whole school is committed, thus providing further continuity.

### Continuity through Common Ground

The final, deeply significant provider of continuity is a set of eight school-wide themes through which content is organized 'vertically'. These themes address 'human commonalities', the common ground of human experience that has relevance for all students, regardless of cultural, linguistic, educational, socio-economic background. A key to the school's vision for international education is, 'The common ground, from multiple perspectives'.

### Collaborative Planning

Teachers at all grade levels and in all learning areas work collaboratively to develop units of learning. It is in the context of these units that conceptual content, standards, assessments and activities come together as integrated, meaning-ful learning. ESL and 'learning support' teachers are integral members of these planning teams and work to ensure access for all learners.

### Control with Creativity

The school's curriculum provides a clear and common framework for learning, thus offering guarantees of access to learners, but carefully avoids the constraints on creativity that can plague more 'bureaucratic' curriculum providers.

### Complete Coherence

The ISB curriculum model, for which the current working title is, 'The Common Ground Curriculum' offers a comprehensive, connected learning framework, driven by a simple yet powerful mission, with shared outcomes, clear standards, character education, a coherent thematic framework of 'common ground' content, collaborative planning and school-wide continuity of learning. From the school's perspective it represents the most satisfying response to date to the challenge of defining and delivering 'an international education'.

This school's commitment to inclusion is evident, not only in its mission statement, 'everyone included, challenged and successful', but also in the fact that it has invested heavily in making this mantra a reality. All staff are involved in ongoing 'professional learning', the school's umbrella term for professional appraisal and development. These systems are embedded in common agreements as to what inclusion, challenge and success 'look like' in the classroom. Professional development includes partici-pation in on-site Learning Institutes, consisting of a week of workshops and year of reflective follow-up with learning partners. These in turn are related to variable pay systems, so that as teachers learn more, they earn more. ISB is the only school I know of that actually gives financial incentives to teachers who are on ECIS subject com-mittees. Further evidence of their commitment to ESL students is the high number of staff that has received training in ESL and language acquisition.

The ISB's programmes are certainly valid options to PYP and MYP schools. The challenge for parents is finding effective options such as these.

The importance of finding a school that has enlightened leadership, an inclusive curriculum and a pedagogical approach that is open to all cultures cannot be over-emphasised.

## Conclusion

This chapter has looked at the importance of being aware of power relations in education. Three pedagogical approaches were considered and it was determined that a Transformative Pedagogical approach is better suited to second language learners in that it affirms the identity of all learners through collaborative Critical Inquiry. The argument that the IBO programmes adhere to progressive critical theories was presented as was the idea that the programme could perhaps be strengthened by adding more 'action' components to ensure that teachers and students are truly working in the spirit of international mindedness and towards concrete goals grounded in our social realities and those of the broader society.

It was stressed how parents must be informed to help them choose the right school for their child and this is one of the main purposes of this book. Parents need to be aware of the power imbalance that can exist in schools. Children and parents need to know that their language and culture is not inferior to any other. Sometimes though, when International Schools exclude other languages, the message they are giving is that the only language that matters is English, and other languages and cultures are inferior. This will only change when the policy makers and decision makers become more informed and dedicated in their commitment to Internationalism.

### Implications for parents

- Be aware of the role politics can play in education.
- Become involved in the life of the school.
- Share information about your child and your culture with the school.
- Select a school that has visionary leadership.
- Do not choose a school that follows a skills-based approach to learning, this does not work for ESL learners.
- Understand the school's approach to literacy.
- Do not choose a school that has an English-only approach.
- Speak out against discriminative practices in school and also inform your embassy, company, the IBO and CIS.
- Do not accept that your child has to be placed in courses that are streamed or tracked (this goes totally against the idea of inclusionary practice).
- Learn what the teachers' beliefs about teaching are.
- Be sure that your child is in a caring environment.
- Check that your child has abundant opportunities to learn through collaboration.
- Know what the learning goals are.
- Make sure your child's identity is fully recognised and respected.

- Do not keep your child in a school where you are not able to have a coherent dialogue on all issues with both teachers and administration.

## Implications for teachers
- Know your identity as a teacher.
- Be conscious of the role of politics in education.
- Ask for staff development in second language acquisition.
- Speak out against a curriculum that does not meet the needs of L2 learners.
- Know the children you teach, where they come from, what languages they speak and to whom; learn about their life experiences, try to build these into your lessons, understand what their difficulties with English are.
- Respect the children by allowing them to make good use of their L1 in the classroom context.
- Look out for cultural bias in standardised tests.
- Use tasks that encourage children to think critically.
- Create opportunities for interaction and collaboration.
- Speak out against discriminative practices.
- Share knowledge with your colleagues.
- Be an advocate for change.
- Involve ESL parents in dialogue, especially about ongoing classroom matters, don't wait for parent/teacher appointments to talk to them.
- Build Ada's framework for Critical Literacy into your teaching.
- Inform the IBO or accreditation authorities of unethical events or malpractice.
- Challenge misinformed leaders.
- Remember you have a choice in how you work with ESL children. Choose to involve them, choose to know them and choose to respect them.

## Notes
1. A Scripted Curriculum requires teachers to read verbatim what has been written by the education authority.
2. Fair assessment of the second language child requires testing material that relates to the child's community, culture and individual characteristics. ESL children should be assessed in their stronger language, not in the L2 as often happens. Standardised tests are often norm referenced, i.e. they may compare the student to L1 speakers of English, and thus give misleading results when applied to ESL children. They are often paper and pencil tests that have multiple choice answers and as such they do not measure the different aspects of language that the ESL child may have acquired nor do they test knowledge of the curriculum.

## Chapter 2

# Research, Theory and Good Practice

## Introduction

ESL students are faced with the challenge of learning a new language and, at the same time, of having to learn in that language. It requires more linguistic skills to use language for academic purposes than it does for everyday conversation. ESL children need to know both at the same time.

This chapter looks at what International Education can learn from recent research and theory on second language acquisition. The difference between conversational and academic fluency is discussed, as is the length of time it takes to develop both in the school context. The way an ESL child uses both her languages to improve her understanding is presented and the impact of recent brain research on pedagogy is considered.

The theories of Collier and Thomas, Cummins, Halliday, Krashen and Vygotsky are presented and their relevance to International Education is discussed. Practical suggestions are made for planning and organising instruction so that ESL children can participate and develop their academic language proficiency in all areas of the curriculum.

In conclusion, implications of the research and theory are proposed for both educators and parents.

## How Students Acquire Conversational and Academic Fluency

Research (e.g. Collier & Thomas, 1997; Cummins, 1981; Hakuta *et al.*, 2000; Klesmer, 1994) has shown that second language students acquire considerable fluency in the dominant language of society when they are exposed to it in the environment and at school. Collier and Thomas' 1997 research among middle-class immigrant students, taught exclusively through English in the Fairfax County district of the USA, suggested that a period of 5 to 10 years is required for students to catch up with their L1 English speaking peers. ESL children in many International School contexts may be exposed to English only when they are at school. However, it is generally observed that these students achieve considerable fluency in about two years. Despite this rapid growth in conversational fluency though, it generally takes a minimum of five to seven years for second language children to catch up with their L1 English speaking peers in academic aspects of language.

### BICS and CALP

In the early 1980s Jim Cummins coined the terms BICS and CALP. These acronyms are still often used by ESL teachers in International Schools. BICS stands for *Basic Interpersonal Communicative Skills*. In other words, the skills needed to converse in social situations such as in everyday, straightforward conversational communication where the speakers may use gestures and communication is aided by contextual support. CALP stands for *Cognitive Academic Language Proficiency*. These refer to the academic language skills that ESL students need in order to be able to deal with the academic demands of the mainstream curriculum. The level of language in the classroom is academically demanding and is often abstract and lacking in contextual support such as gestures, real objects and face-to-face interaction.

## Rationale behind BICS and CALP definition

Cummins' initial reason for making the distinction between conversational fluency and academic language proficiency came from his discussions with school psychologists. They were concerned that there could be a bias in the assessments they used with bilingual children. An analysis of more that 400 teacher referral forms and psychological assessments by these psychologists revealed that children who were still in the process of acquiring English were being recommended by teachers for testing. The assumption that teachers made was that, because the children's oral skills (BICS) were so good, they should be doing better in class and, as this was not the case, they must have remedial learning problems.

This often occurs in International Schools. For example, I recently visited an International School with small class sizes, a pupil–teacher ratio of 12:1, that employed two full-time ESL teachers and four full-time special needs teachers. Discussion with the administration and the head of special needs revealed that students often attended ESL classes for one or two years, were then placed in the mainstream and when they didn't cope they were referred to the special needs teachers. The special needs department admitted they were not sure that all the students they were working with truly had a learning disability. The ESL teachers believed their job was complete once the children were talking: it was up to the mainstream teachers to deliver the curriculum.

This school needed professional development on second language acquisition for all its teachers and administrators and both ESL and special needs teachers needed up to date professional development in their subject areas. It was apparent that the school would benefit from reshuffling its staff so that they would have four full-time ESL teachers and two special needs teachers rather than vice versa. Many of the students had been referred for testing in their first year of learning English and the language of the test was English. This should not happen but it often does. This was a school that wanted to do well by all its children. However, they did not have a real understanding of the specific needs of the ESL child. While it is important that teachers be on the look out for children with learning difficulties, it is equally important not to consider as being remedial those children who have not yet acquired the skills to deal fully with the mainstream.

## BICS/CALP Definitions Raise Awareness of the Difficulties L2 Learners Face

Another thing to bear in mind is that there is no predetermined sequential order to children acquiring BICS and CALP. For the most part children will become fluent before being able to deal fully with the academic registers of the curriculum. However, there are many students, often from Asian backgrounds, who have learnt to read and write English in a scholarly manner but who do not know how to speak English and so their BICS lag behind their CALP.

The idea that it normally takes about two years to achieve conversational fluency does not mean that academic tasks should be put on hold until the child acquires fluency. The ESL child must be involved in the mainstream life of the classroom from her very first day and classroom tasks modified to suit her linguistic abilities.

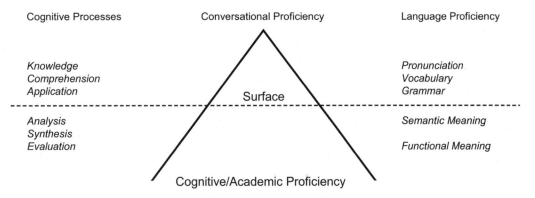

**Figure 3** The Cummins iceberg
*Source*: Baker (2003: 170)

In Figure 3 the distinction between BICS and CALP is seen in the image of an iceberg. Above the surface are skills such as comprehension and speaking. Underneath the surface are the skills of analysis and synthesis. Above the surface are the language skills of pronunciation, vocabulary and grammar. Below the surface are deeper subtle language skills of meaning and creative composition.

The BICS/CALP distinction helps to explain why children fail when they are withdrawn from ESL support after a couple of years and left to deal with the mainstream curriculum on their own. This is a common scenario in some less effective International Schools. We cannot assume that, just because children have achieved surface fluency, their CALP has developed enough to deal with the demands of the curriculum. The BICS/CALP definition also points out clearly why every teacher in an International School is an ESL teacher. Without the mainstream teachers' help, ESL children will find it difficult to flourish in mainstream subject areas.

There are criticisms of the BICS/CALP theory (for more on this see Baker, 2003). Harley *et al.* (1990) suggest that a bilingual's language competencies are evolving, dynamic, interacting and intricate. They are not easily compartmentalised into two stages. This is true. However Cummins' definitions have heightened awareness of the difficulties children face when learning in academic settings.

## Instructional implications of CALP for teachers

Cummins proposes that teachers think of the instructional implications of CALP as being made up of three components: cognitive, academic and language.

(1) *Cognitive* – Instruction should be cognitively challenging using thinking skills such as evaluating inferring, generalising and classifying.
(2) *Academic* – Curriculum content should be integrated with language instruction so that students learn the language of specific academic areas.
(3) *Language* – Critical language awareness must be developed both linguistically and socio-culturally/socio-politically. Children need to be made aware of the different status and power that are projected with language and language use. They should also be encouraged to compare and contrast grammar, cognates, etc. in English and their mother-tongue.

## Two languages work together to improve understanding

Bilingualism and multilingualism are possible because the brain can store multiple languages (Baker, 2003). Although a child may have several languages, there is one integrated place for thought. When a child is taught the concept of, for example, 'habitat' in one language, the concept does not need to be taught again in the other languages of the child. When a bilingual child is taught how to use a dictionary at school she is able to explain how to use it in her mother-tongue even though she was not explicitly taught that skill in her L1.

Cummins explains this theory in his *Common Underlying Proficiency* (CUP) model. This model is illustrated in Figure 4.

In Figure 4 two icebergs are seen above the surface level. In outward conversation the two languages are often separate. Below the surface, where the internal processing and the storage of the languages happen, words and images are stored separately in the two languages. However, there is also a common area where the icebergs blend or melt together in a central unified processing system. Cummins says that it is in this area that Common Underlying Proficiency resides. Both languages can use this system. Understandings, concepts and processing share this common ground in the brain and both languages have access to it.

Important implications of the CUP theory:

- It does not matter what languages a child is working in, the thoughts that accompany her writing and reading come from the same central source.
- Speaking, listening, reading or writing in the first or second language helps develop the child's whole cognitive system.

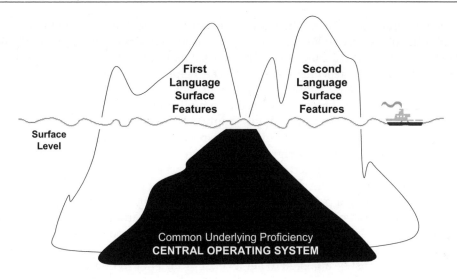

Figure 4   The Cummins dual iceberg
*Source*: Baker (2003: 165)

- If both languages are not working fully, perhaps because the school has an English-only policy for example, cognitive and academic performance may be hurt.

(For a fuller discussion on this see Baker (2003) and Cummins (2004).)

Cummins stresses that it is essential for the ESL child's central language proficiency to be well developed. Rather than one language interfering with the development of the other (a myth frequently believed in International Education) this joining of languages beneath the surface in the operating area of the brain provides social advantages, thinking advantages and cultural advantages in the long term.

## Relevance of CUP theory for international education

The implication here for International Schools is that teachers should actively encourage children to make associations between languages and point out similarities and differences. Parents and older students can be used as a valuable resource. Policies that discourage the use of the child's mother-tongue may harm her overall cognitive growth.

## Planning for developing CALP

Children face many different contexts in schools. Each curriculum area uses different communication mechanisms that demand different skills of the children. Each class differs in the subject and the complexity of the language and also in the style the teacher uses. Compare a history class studying the Second World War with a physical education class where the child is learning how to serve in tennis. In the PE class individual words and actions are enough to get the teacher's meaning across. An understanding of the complexities of the Second World War cannot be transmitted through single words and actions. Therefore the teaching of content material requires that the teacher uses a *scaffolding approach* to the teaching of her subject – helping ESL children understand by building on their existing knowledge and by using visuals, objects, eye contact, clues and cues. This is called context embedded communication.

International School teachers cannot simply rely on the text or workbook to get their meaning across to ESL children. Texts, especially at a secondary level, are often just words divided up into paragraphs on a page. Imagine the situation of an ESL child in a secondary class faced with such a text and a teacher who simply delivers a lecture on the subject. The child is left hearing a string of words looking at a large collection of words on a page and understanding very little.

This is an example of context-reduced communication and unfortunately it is an experience well known to ESL children in International Schools where teachers do not know how to deliver their subject to ESL learners. The type of communication an ESL child needs must be adjusted to her level of proficiency in English. The lower the child's proficiency, the more context embedded material is needed. As her language proficiency increases, context-reduced communication becomes possible.

Cummins (2004) has developed a framework, depicted in Figure 5, which can help teachers with their planning and programme design.

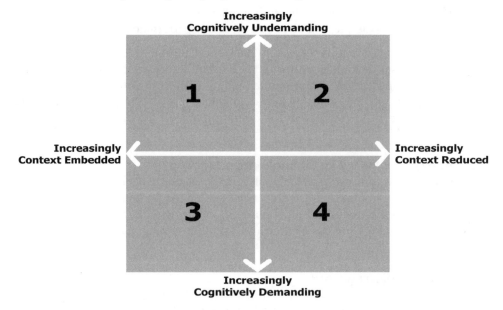

**Figure 5**  Range of contextual support and degree of cognitive involvement in language tasks and activities

*Source*: Cummins (2004: 68)

In Cummins' model the upper quadrants represent cognitively undemanding communication – simple language containing relatively small amounts of information to be processed. Going down the vertical axis to the lower quadrants, communication becomes progressively more cognitively demanding, language is more complex and greater amounts of information are being transmitted.

Going along the horizontal axis from left to right the amount of context embedded in communication reduces – less support and fewer clues are being provided to help understanding.

Informal conversation is a typical quadrant 1 activity whereas a quadrant 2 activity might be copying notes from the board or doing worksheets. Quadrants 3 and 4 contain more cognitively demanding activities. Debating a point of view would be a quadrant 3 activity while writing an essay would fall into quadrant 4. Language in the classroom can vary from the 'here and now', 'face-to-face' experiences of quadrant 1, to the context-reduced, 'you are all on your own' writing, reading and testing experiences of quadrant 4.

The intention is not that ESL students remain in the higher, undemanding quadrants but rather that they progress towards cognitively demanding activities with the correct amount of contextual help. They should be given more exposure to quadrant 3 activities than may be necessary for L1 speakers of English.

The quadrant can be used by teachers to discuss the difficulty of given tasks in order to provide students with the contextual supports needed to complete the task successfully. Instruction for cognitive academic growth will move from 1–3–4 with quadrant 2 activities being included from time to time for reinforcement or practice.

Pauline Gibbons (1995, 1998) suggests a similar progression. She distinguishes three stages where children move from context embedded to context reduced work. They are:

- small group work          *quadrant 1*
- teacher guided reporting   *quadrant 3*
- journal writing            *quadrant 4*

Mainstream teachers interested in creating tasks that develop a collaborative use of language will find a wealth of ideas in Gibbons' book, *Scaffolding Language, Scaffolding Learning* (2002).

Cummins' quadrant can also be a useful tool for examining an ESL child's portfolio to observe the progression of the child through the quadrants and to determine the level of task she is ready to cope with. It can also be used effectively to explain the nature of tasks to parents and point out clearly the proficiency level of their child.

## The Importance of Talk for Language Acquisition

Talk is fundamental in a class of second language learners. ESL children need to hear a lot of talk in order to learn how to talk themselves and they need lots of opportunities to interact in varied contexts. However, beginning ESL children should not be forced to talk; rather they should be encouraged to participate by listening and observing until they themselves feel ready to talk. Parents are also advised not to insist on their children speaking English if the child is not prepared to do so. Parents have sometimes told me that when they ask their child to communicate in English, perhaps for the benefit of an Anglophone invited to their home, the child refuses. This is quite natural and normal. The child does not want to 'perform' in her second language. The child will use her language in the context of natural communication when she has a real purpose for talking and when she can communicate a message efficiently in that language. Teachers need to create such contexts in their classrooms.

## Immersion research

Research (Swain, 1995) on language acquisition in French Bilingual Immersion Programmes in Canada found that interaction, and especially talk produced by the children themselves, was a crucial factor for language development (Immersion Bilingual Education is schooling where children are taught through a second majority language). The research found that although children developed fluency in French (their L2), many did not achieve full proficiency and their grammar was not fully accurate even after several years of hearing French in classrooms where French was used for learning other subjects. Swain suggests that this is because the children had very little opportunity for extended discourse. In other words, they had little chance to speak (produce) long stretches of French in the classroom and were often simply required to give minimal answers.

We now know that producing language encourages children to process the language more deeply (Allen *et al.*, 1990; Swain, 1995). We learn to talk by talking and we talk when we have a reason to do so. The way we talk depends on the context we are in. When we have a meeting with our boss, the way we talk is different from the way we talk when chatting with our partners, children or friends. In their own language ESL children may know how to adapt talk depending on who they talk to and where they are, but they need to be taught how to do this in English

In the classroom context they need to have authentic purposes for their talk. Some authentic reasons for talk are:

- *asking and receiving information*
  - ✎ e.g. students are required to ask for information in order to complete a task;
- *expressing feelings and ideas*
  - ✎ e.g. students are encouraged to express their feelings on various topics they are interested in;
- *getting to know someone in both formal and informal situations*
  - ✎ e.g. students are taught the appropriateness of different types of language;
- *clarifying thoughts*
  - ✎ e.g. students need to be given the opportunities to think through their learning by talking with their peers and with the teacher;
- *communicating knowledge*
  - ✎ e.g. students need opportunities to share what they know with others;

- *questioning understanding*
  ✤ e.g. students need to be encouraged to question what is presented to them.

ESL children need to use English in as many different contexts and for as many different reasons as possible. It is only through experiences that they will acquire the rules and conventions of spoken English. Teachers need to provide occasions for children to talk about topics, subjects and tasks in various circumstances – as a whole class, in small groups and in pairs. They need to ask questions that require stretches of language rather than one-word answers.

One way of doing this is to set up problem solving tasks that encourage group and peer discussion. Teachers can also set up situations where the ESL children are the experts, the ones with the knowledge to share. When the goal of the lesson is communication in order to complete a task, it is important that teachers focus on how effective the child is at getting her message across rather than on grammatical accuracy. It is an idea to jot down frequent or repeated errors and do a mini lesson on correct forms later, relating the errors to the context of the lesson. It is important not to intervene and block communication when the child is engaged in talking.

Teachers must also give ESL children plenty of time to answer questions. It is important to bear in mind that ESL children are trying to come to terms with a new language and are not only learning how to speak, they are also learning what is appropriate to say.

A classroom environment that is supportive of ESL learners is a natural learning environment where the teacher has planned units built around themes that are of genuine interest to children. The focus is on interaction: students talking about their reading and writing, talking through tasks. Learning occurs by assisted performance in the context of a joint activity. This socio-cultural approach to learning is based on the work of Vygotsky (1978). We now know that participation with others to complete a task develops cognition. Lev Vygotsky (1978: 25) expresses this well:

> A child's speech is as important as the role of action in attaining the goal. Children not only speak about what they are doing: their speech and action are part of one and the same psychological function directed toward the solution of the problem at hand. The more complex the action demanded by the situation and the less direct its solution, the greater the importance played by speech in the operation as a whole.

## Brain Research

For many years now it has been accepted that children learn best by making and doing. An example could be learning through an active experience such as writing a story for younger learners and then sharing that story with them. Recent research on the brain supports this view. The human brain contains billions of nerve cells called neurons. Dendrites on the neurons (finger-like branches of the nerve cells) provide receptive surfaces that create connections between neurons and transmit information from one to the other.

Scientists used to believe that each person was born with a certain number of brain cells and therefore that a person's intellect was something predetermined genetically. Recent research refutes this idea and suggests that much of the wiring of the brain's neurons comes after birth and depends on the experiences children have. It is now believed that the brain is formed at least in part by the environment. We now know that the brain is plastic at birth and not rigid as previously believed. It has the ability to change chemistry and structure in response to the environment. Brain researchers now believe that intelligence is determined, amongst other factors, by:

- the environment;
- nutrition;
- prior learning;
- life experiences;
- beliefs;
- values.

The brain can grow new dendrites. Dendrites form connections between neurons that create memory and learning. Chains of neurons form when children make connections with learning. Sousa (1998) suggests that brain research has five implications for education:

(1)    The brain makes more neural connections when it is actively engaged in learning, therefore learning should be multi-sensory and interactive.
        ✍ In other words, children in interactive language classrooms who talk through their learning, who are given authentic reasons to talk about topics and who use drama and art to express their ideas, will be better able to remember the content of the lesson.

(2)    Activities that involve emotion-release chemicals in the brain that strengthen memory. Thus it is important that learning is made meaningful to children.
        ✍ In other words, using humour and emotion can make language learning fun, meaningful and memorable.

(3)    The human brain is constantly striving to make patterns and create connections so learning should be built on prior knowledge.
        ✍ In other words, using the child's home language and eliciting prior knowledge and background knowledge helps the child to make sense of her learning.

(4)    The brain works through a hierarchy of tasks. It starts with physical survival then moves to emotional survival and only then does it turn to thinking and learning. This means that students must feel physically safe and emotionally secure before they are able to learn.
        ✍ In other words, children need a classroom environment where they feel safe to try out new language and take risks with using that language without worrying about getting everything correct.

(5)  Students today are used to environmental stimuli that are rapidly changing such as television and computer screens. Students are constantly taking in a lot more information than in the past.

  ↳ In other words, this suggest that short bursts of learning are more effective than long class periods.

Teachers need to create experience-based opportunities for children to learn. The more involved children become in the experience, the more dendrites are created. Interactive classrooms offer more experiences than classrooms that follow Traditional Pedagogy. Experiences create natural reasons for talking and therefore more varied interactional speech patterns occur. The child learns to talk by talking through the task in hand and relating it to relevant experiences.

Learning to speak English cannot be a task that is relegated to the English classroom or the ESL class. If second language children are to be successful in school they need to be in natural learning environments that are experience-based and language-focused throughout the whole curriculum. Collaborative learning activities, where children work in small groups or pairs to complete meaningful tasks that give them the opportunity to express their ideas, beliefs and identities, should be common practice. We now know that language is learnt best when it is used for genuine communication purposes.

## Communicative Methodology and its Influence on Education

Those who studied languages in the 1960s and 1970s left school able to read a little and write a little of the foreign language studied. Maybe some grammatical structures were learnt and even how to say a few phrases by heart, for example the classic, *la plume de ma tante*. However, no idea how to use such phrases in different contexts was taught – in fact the phrases often made little or no sense outside the classroom. Teachers and applied linguists realised that this approach, known as Traditional Pedagogy, was not working; students were often structurally competent in the language but did not know how to use it effectively to express their needs.

In the early 1970s, the Council of Europe convened a team of experts to study language in a new way by looking closely at what were the language needs of various groups of learners. They studied the different situations in which language is used and came up with a list of functions or uses of language (van Ek, 1975). There was a shift from teaching language through a structural (grammatical) syllabus to a semantic (meaning-based) syllabus. Linguists developed syllabi that contained lists of uses or functions.

However teachers realised that something else was needed. Children had to be taught the skill of communication. The early 1980s saw the birth of the communicative methodology and students in language classes were taught how to communicate effectively in different situational and social contexts. Linguists had developed the theory that language is best learnt when it is used for genuine communicative purposes. This new approach to teaching language influenced teaching in general. Collaborative learning, a strategy used in Progressive Pedagogy, was born out of the communicative methodology. A crucial feature of the communicative method is that it operates with stretches of language above the sentence level, using language in real situations (although these situations often had to be simulated in the classroom). Teachers strove to create a classroom that was rich in talk so that students could interact, explore, think, question and express themselves. In order for this to happen, teachers and linguists realised that students needed a supportive, anxiety-free atmosphere. Stephen Krashen introduced such an idea in the early 1980s.

## The influence of Stephen Krashen

Stephen Krashen is probably one of the linguists most responsible for the changes that have occurred in language teaching over the past decades. We will take a look at three of his theories and their implications for ESL students.

### The affective filter theory

The word 'affective' comes from the noun 'affect' – meaning feeling or emotion. Krashen (Krashen & Terrell, 1983) states that emotions and feelings can determine how easily language is acquired. The affective filter is a metaphor that describes how a learner's attitudes can affect the success of language acquisition. Emotional states such as learning anxiety, stress, low self-confidence and lack of motivation are like a filter that acts as a barrier to effective language acquisition.

Krashen believes we need states of low anxiety, low stress and high motivation for optimal language acquisition to occur. This agrees with the brain research findings mentioned earlier: learning is more effective when students feel physically and emotionally secure (see Figure 6).

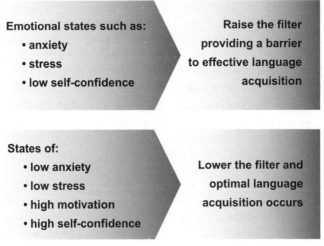

**Figure 6**  The affective filter
*Source*: Krashen and Terrell (1983)

Imagine being an 11-year-old child sitting in a class full of children who don't speak your language. The teacher (who speaks only English) is reading from a textbook. You have a copy of the text in front of you. The only words that you can read are the small words such as 'is', 'the', 'and'. Nothing makes any sense to you, not what the teacher is saying nor the words written on the page. Imagine the state of anxiety of a child in such a situation. This kind of textbook-driven classroom is still common in some International Schools. ESL children can find themselves in the above situation for extended periods of time, day in and day out. School administrators and special subject teachers need to realise that being submersed in a 'context-reduced' situation like the one described above will not make understanding happen. ESL children need language delivered at a level they can understand.

*Comprehensible input*

Krashen suggests that language acquisition requires comprehensible input, that is, clues to what the language that is being taught means. His theory is based on the assumption that first and second language acquisition take place in similar ways. We know that children do not pick up their first language simply by listening and mimicking the sounds around them. They need caring parents who repeat utterances over and over again. Parents instinctively provide the child with a model of correct speech, explaining and showing by example how to communicate. They correct in such a way that the child doesn't realise she is being corrected.

Krashen (Krashen & Terrell, 1983) believes that the ESL child needs language input that consists of the new language along with the clues to what the language means. The clues are fundamental – without them the child could hear great stretches of language without ever learning to understand it (just like the imaginary 11 year old mentioned earlier).

Comprehensible input is the kind of language that parents use naturally with their children. It is slower and simpler. It focuses on the here and now. The meaning is more important than the form. It extends and builds on the child's existing language base. This is how successful language teachers interact with their students. Krashen states that the most effective sort of comprehensible input is that which is just slightly beyond the learner's current level of competence. If the input is too easy or too difficult it does not promote improvement. This concept is sometimes expressed as $i + 1$ (where $i$ is the current competency and $+ 1$ gives the notion of just beyond the current competency level). Teachers working with ESL children need to adjust their language to the needs of the learner. They need to express language in a way that it can be understood. Drama, visuals and concrete demonstrations should be used to make abstract concepts comprehensible. Teachers also need to create authentic reasons for children to communicate with each other. They should tap into their existing knowledge and move them on from there ($i + 1$). It is also important to focus on the form of the language in a meaningful way such as pointing out similarities and differences between English and the child's mother-tongue.

*Language acquisition and learning*

Krashen (Krashen & Terrell, 1983) also believes that there are two ways of developing ability in a language: acquisition and learning:

- Acquisition is the natural subconscious process of 'soaking up' a language like that of young children developing their first language.
- Learning is a formal, conscious process often involving mastering rules of grammar, vocabulary and spelling.

Krashen believes that acquisition is the most important process in developing second language ability. Certainly the past has shown that formulaic approaches to the teaching of language don't work. Focusing on structures, knowing the names of tenses and so on may well be interesting language study but it does not teach the child to actively use the language. ESL children need to know the language for all the different subject areas and how to use that language effectively.

International School classrooms should provide rich, natural hands-on language experiences to facilitate the natural process of language acquisition. Children should also be made aware that making mistakes is a necessary part of language learning. They need to know that their classroom is a place where the trial and error process is valued. Research confirms that students in classes where comprehensible input strategies are used to teach mainstream subjects acquire impressive amounts of English and learn content matter as well (Krashen & Biber, 1988). But is comprehensible input, on its own, enough?

## Beyond Comprehensible Input

Progressive Pedagogies promote strategies that aim for student involvement and understanding but Cummins (2004) points out that we must go further than this for a deeper understanding to occur. Teachers must work with children on projects that address real social issues and also themes that involve children in realising their identities. Cummins states that for optimal progress to happen, cognitive challenge and intrinsic motivation must be instilled into the interactions between students. He agrees that ESL children need contextual supports built into their programme of studies. These include (Cummins, 2000):

- Stimulating the students' prior knowledge and building background knowledge through their own language where necessary.
- Modifying instruction through paraphrase, repetition, demonstration, gestures and so on.
- Use of graphic organisers to explain concepts (see Chapter 6 for an example of a graphic organiser).
- Hands-on activities in content areas such as science, maths and social studies.
- Cooperative learning and other forms of project work that encourage students to generate new knowledge rather than simply learn information.

- Creative use of technology to promote cultural identities, e.g.:
  - Research using CD-ROM encyclopaedias or the World Wide Web.
  - Word processing and data analysis programmes that can be used as tools for producing reports of project work.
  - Networking with distant classes (even in far away countries) to work together on bilingual projects that seek to tackle and discuss social problems.
  - Use of video cameras to create texts for real audiences.
- Integration of reading and writing in a wide variety of genres with all of the above.

## Preparing children for the real world

Cummins (2004) stresses that a pedagogical approach that involves the above techniques matches the criteria that corporate companies state they desire in their workforce. According to Cummins, companies say they need:

- employees who know how to retrieve information through books, journals and databases;
- employees who know how to critically analyse information;
- employees who know how to assess information and its relevance and worth;
- employees who know how to use information to solve problems;
- employees who know how to work collaboratively with colleagues from a different linguistic and racial background in order to solve problems collectively.

Cummins (2000) proposes that if we interpret this 'job description' as a statement of desired educational outcomes, we can see that it is radically different from the outcomes stated in Traditional Pedagogy. Schools that follow Traditional Pedagogical approaches are generally following a static, skill-based curriculum and probably many of the skills being taught are obsolete for today's workforce.

## Instruction for the development of academic expertise

Cummins (2004) has developed a framework that highlights the importance of teachers focusing on instruction. He identifies the three areas presented in Figure 7.

Academic language proficiency takes time to develop and requires that children be exposed to academic language. This includes attention to the form of the language but also to its meaning and use. ESL children must have opportunities for extensive reading and writing. They also need to be cognitively engaged in challenging tasks and opportunities for the development and expression of their identities.

The following definitions are adapted from Cummins (2001b; 2004).

*Focus on meaning*

The focus on meaning component suggests that Krashen's Comprehensible Input theory is only a starting point. In order to deepen children's understanding of language and content, comprehensible input must be transformed into critical literacy. Ada's Critical Literacy Approach mentioned in Chapter 1 elaborates clearly what a focus on

---

**A. Focus on Meaning**
    Making Input Comprehensible
    Developing Critical Literacy

**B. Focus on Language**
    Awareness of Language Forms and Uses
    Critical Analysis of Language Forms and Uses

**C. Focus on Use**
    Using Language to:
        ▪ Generate New Knowledge
        ▪ Create Literature an Art
        ▪ Act on Social Realities

---

**Figure 7**   A framework for academic language learning
*Source*: Cummins (2004: 274)


meaning is. Students must be able to relate textual and instructional meanings to their own experiences and prior knowledge. They have to be able to critically analyse the information in the text. For example, they need to be able to evaluate the arguments and then use the outcomes of their analysis in an activity that is highly motivating.

*Focus on language*
   By focusing on language Cummins does not intend a return to the 'back-to-basics' approach where language skills are often taught out of context and devoid of any meaning. Rather, in the focus on language component, he includes not only a focus on the formal aspects of language such as phonics and grammar but also a critical awareness of how language operates within society. If students are to participate effectively in society they need to be able not only to 'read the word' but also the 'world'. In other words they need to understand how people use language to arrive at social or political goals.
   Cummins (2001b) suggests the following kinds of activities focus on deepening students' knowledge of language and multilingual issues:

- Looking at the structure of language systems, for example the relationship between sounds and spelling, regional and class-based accents, grammar and vocabulary.
- Exploring the conventions of different musical and literary forms such as rap, poetry, haiku, fictions and ballads.
- Understanding the appropriateness of expression in different contexts such as the cultural conventions of being polite, street language versus school language,

everyday speech compared to the language of books, language variety used as a form of identity in groups.

- Investigating ways of organising oral and written discourse to create powerful or persuasive messages in speeches, political rhetoric, advertising and so on.
- Being aware of the diversity of language use in monolingual and multilingual settings and contexts. Looking at language loss in families and discussing the political implications in the home and broader society. Evaluating the spread of English in the world, and so on.

*Focus on use*

The focus on use component argues that second language acquisition will remain abstract and classroom-bound unless students have the opportunities to express themselves, their identities and their intelligence through the second language. This may be difficult in the early stages and there should be no problem with ESL students drafting revising and editing in their first language. This allows them to develop such skills while joining in the same activity as their peers. Optimal instruction will strive to give students the opportunity to express themselves and their identities through creating knowledge that motivates communication.

Cummins' academic framework is a tool that can be used in International Schools to help administrators and teachers develop a language policy. It should be considered as a starting point for discussion rather than a prescriptive solution. The framework also highlights the fact that teachers have choices. They can choose to go beyond the simple adherence to a handed-down, prescribed curriculum by implementing the standards in ways that acknowledge their students' identities and the 'funds of knowledge' they bring to the classroom. Teachers can choose to involve their ESL students in powerful literacy practices such as those proposed by Ada (see Chapter 1).

The academic framework provides International School educators with a means for studying the curriculum and stretching it in a way that prepares students to become citizens who can make important and meaningful contributions to society. International educators need to explicitly place 'international mindedness' at the core of the curriculum and ensure that the policies in Internationals Schools are consistent with this view.

## Writing Across the Curriculum

The writing demands of the curriculum increase as children progress through school. It is common to find in International Schools ESL children who can read nearly at the same grade level as their English speaking peers (especially if they have maintained literacy in their mother-tongues) but whose performance in writing is much below the grade level of those peers. The reasons for this have been discussed in detail earlier but it is perhaps worth summarising some of the key issues that cause ESL children to lag behind their peers in writing:

- We have looked at Cummins' work which explains the length of time needed for ESL children to be able to deal with the academic demands of the curriculum.
- We have considered the importance of a stress-free environment proposed by Krashen.
- We have compared Traditional, Progressive and Transformative Pedagogies and suggested that Transformative Pedagogy is of paramount importance to ESL learners: it leads to furthering self-identity and ultimately to their acquiring knowledge that they can put into action.
- We have examined the importance of teachers focusing on 'meaning', 'language' and 'use' with emphasis on developing Critical Literacy and have argued that this, alongside teachers valuing and affirming students' identity, is crucial to effective pedagogy for ESL learners.

Cummins (2004) has argued that there is a need for more formal instruction in the structures of language and conventions of writing if ESL students are to break the academic code of the curriculum. However, teaching language explicitly does not mean a return to the teaching of grammar in isolation and meaningless drills (as stressed earlier). Nor does it mean the compartmentalising of the timetable into spelling, reading, writing, grammar and so on. It does mean, however, that students are encouraged to reflect on how language is used in authentic situations for a range of purposes and audiences. This means that students must understand the meaning of Genre. In other words they need to understand the way in which language changes depending on the context and on the purpose it is being used for.

## The Genre Theory

The genre approach to teaching writing comes from the work of Michael Halliday and other Australian systemic functional linguists. Systemic functional linguistics is an approach to grammar developed by Halliday that sees language in a social context. It views language as a means of communication and not as a set of rules.

Halliday's (1975) research has shown that children learn language not just by being immersed in it but also by interacting with other people, especially the adults who look after them. The role the adult plays is crucial to the child's development. The adult, by rephrasing, clarifying and extending the child's utterances, provides a model for the child. Adult and child collaborate to make sense of the utterance and build meaning together. This agrees with both the Krashen and Vvgotsky views of a joint construction approach to language acquisition mentioned earlier.

### What is genre?

The genres of spoken and written English are specific to English culture. ESL children may well know the features of different genres in their own languages (because genre is culture specific) but they need to be explicitly taught English genres. Some of the most common genres used in school are:

- discussion;
- explanation;
- narrative;
- procedure;
- recount;
- report.

Each of these genres uses language differently and each genre has certain features that conform to certain patterns. These patterns need to be taught to ESL learners so they can break into the academic code, which is necessary for them to be successful in the upper levels of schooling. Each genre has a distinctive structure that can be found in all texts belonging to that genre. Linguists call this its schematic structure. Teachers can teach the schematic structures and the linguistic forms that are relevant to their subject area. By doing this they are openly showing children the type of writing necessary to be successful in their classrooms.

Science teachers can show students how to write an information report and the procedural writing necessary for effective lab reports. History teachers need to teach children how to write an argument, an explanation and a discussion. Teachers need to find well-written texts and explicitly point out the structure and the linguistic forms that are inherent to the text type. Teachers cannot take for granted that children know how to do such things as 'write an argument for . . .'. They need to know what exactly the teacher means by argument and how this is presented in English.

Mainstream teachers cannot assume that the teaching of writing is the task of the English teacher alone. This poses a problem though: subject teachers implicitly know the features of the genres they teach but they may not be aware of them formally. This means that they may have difficulty explaining to students exactly what it is they want from them. Collaboration with the ESL teacher is crucial here. There is also the very good professional staff development programme, ESL in the Mainstream (DECS, 1999) that dedicates 2 out of its 10 units to the genre approach. For a thorough evaluation of this programme see Carder (2007). Figure 8 illustrates the principal aspects of genre.

Many International Schools have now built a genre approach into the teaching of writing across the curriculum. They have recognised its importance, not only for second language learners, but for all children. ESL parents are urged, when choosing a school and its curriculum for their child, to ask whether the school uses a genre approach to writing.

A word of caution is necessary here. It is common in curriculum documents to find a list of literary forms referred to as genres. Such forms may refer to poetry, plays and novels, as genre types. The genre approach however, refers to the ways things are achieved in a specific culture. Each genre has a specific purpose, a particular structure and specific linguistic features as summarised in Figure 8. These genres are shared by members of a culture and they need to be taught to novices in that culture. If the genre approach to writing is in use in an International School there is more probability

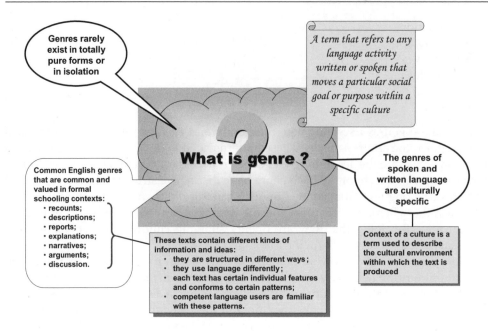

**Figure 8**  Introduction to genre
*Source*: Adapted from DECS (1999)

of children mastering the academic language required for success in the mainstream curriculum.

## Reading for Understanding Across the Curriculum

Research has shown that being able to read in one's own language is one of the most important factors in learning to read in a second language (Cummins, 2001b). Cummins' research revealed that children who have strong first language academic skills when they start learning English tend to go on to attain higher levels of academic achievement across all subject areas. A strong emphasis on maintaining and developing literacy in the L1 is crucial to the ESL child's whole cognitive development.

There has been debate as to which language reading should be introduced in; the mother-tongue or the second language. Cummins suggests there is no formula for this. However, he points out that in most cases it makes good sense to introduce reading in the language the child is most familiar with. Italian and Spanish for example have a more regular sound symbol relationship than English. The 26 letters of the English alphabet are used to represent 44 different sounds or phonemes. Individual letters represent a number of sounds and at other times letters are not pronounced at all. If the child is a native Italian speaker, introducing reading in Italian with its simpler–letter sound relationship may make more sense.

There are significant advantages in having the child reading and writing in both her languages by the end of Grade 2. When this happens the child's identity is strengthened in both languages and she learns to use both her languages to help in her understanding of the curriculum. This extends both languages and cognitive development. In other words, when the two languages are promoted together, each language enriches the other.

## The Reading Process

In Traditional Pedagogy and in the 'back-to-basics' approach to the teaching of reading, much emphasis is placed on decoding the written word. However, according to Edwards, when researchers started analysing the strategies that fluent readers use they discovered that something more complex than decoding word by word was taking place (Edwards, 1995). By listening to children reading aloud researchers discovered that we use our knowledge of life, language and experience to make sense of our reading. Our prior knowledge helps us to predict what is coming next in the text. Successful readers use three cueing systems to help them interpret the written word. These are semantic, syntactic and graphophonic:

- semantic cues draw on the reader's knowledge of meaning;
- syntactic cues use the reader's knowledge of grammar rules to help her decide if the word is correct;
- graphophonic cues require that the reader has a knowledge of the sound system and of the way that sound is represented in writing.

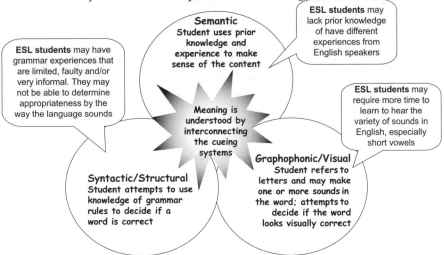

**Figure 9** The three cueing systems
*Source*: CAL (2000: 27)

The three circles in Figure 9 show the three cueing systems that successful readers use to arrive at understanding a written text. ESL children need support in using the three cueing systems because

- they may lack the prior knowledge to access the semantic cueing system. This may affect not only their comprehension but also their motivation to read;
- they may take longer to master the grammar rules they need to decide if a particular word is right in the overall syntax (word-order of the sentence).

ESL teachers used to believe that their students needed to have strong oral skills before they were introduced to reading in the L2. However, today teachers are aware of the importance of developing literacy skills alongside oral skills. Children who arrive in International Schools with no experience of reading in any language are often able to recognise print they see in the environment such as that found in signs (Stop, Underground, McDonald's, and so on). A classroom that is rich in print will help the beginning ESL child with vocabulary building and word recognition.

Teachers need to be aware that children who are already literate in their mother-tongue can transfer their existing skills to English. However, it is important for teachers to familiarise themselves with the literacy practices of the children in their classes. This can help to identify areas of misunderstanding. If for example the child is used to reading from right to left at home the teacher needs to be aware of this. When she has such information the teacher can listen to the child reading in the L1 using her finger to follow the direction and then, in turn, read to the child in English using her finger to show the reverse direction. This gives a clear message to the child that both languages are valued whilst at the same time identifying important differences.

The English mother-tongue speakers in international classrooms are familiar with the literacy practices used in those classrooms. ESL children are not. ESL parents need to be told explicitly the school's view of reading and the ways they can help develop literacy in their child. Teachers who go out of their way to gather information from the child and her parents about the child's mother-tongue reading experience demonstrate that they value the knowledge the child brings to the classroom.

## Children Learn to Read by Reading

Krashen (2004) suggests that the knowledge gained through reading in the L1 can make second language input much more comprehensible. He also suggests that a pleasure reader in the L1 will be a pleasure reader in the second language too. In his book *The Power of Reading* Krashen (2004) tells us that when children read for pleasure they acquire a large vocabulary and they develop the ability to understand and use complex constructions. They also develop a good writing style and become good (but not necessarily perfect) spellers. Krashen argues that second language learners need specific time in the school timetable for 'Free Voluntary Reading'. This means a time that is set aside for reading that does not involve the child having to respond to the reading by, for example, writing a book report or doing vocabulary exercises or answering comprehension questions. The child simply reads for a given period of time. She is encouraged to read what she would like to read, putting down a book if she doesn't like it and choosing another one. Free Voluntary Reading is not intended to replace the literacy or language programmes in schools. Rather, it is meant to complement them. Krashen cites research that demonstrates that in 38 out of 41 studies children practicing Free Voluntary Reading did as well as or better in reading comprehension tests than students given traditional skill-based reading instruction only. Krashen (2004) sums up the skill-based approach in two points:

- skill building means consciously learning a rule, word-meaning or spelling and then making that rule automatic through output practice;
- error correction: once a mistake is corrected students are expected to adjust their conscious knowledge of the rule, word or spelling.

Krashen (2004) argues that language is too vast and too complex to be taught one rule at a time. He emphasises that literacy development can occur without formal instruction. Research by Foertsch (1992) and by Nagy *et al.* (1985) revealed that Free Voluntary Reading often gives better results to direct instruction on tests of reading comprehension, vocabulary, writing and grammar. Krashen points out that in schools that follow Traditional Pedagogy poor readers often don't get to read as much as stronger readers. The children who read well are given more opportunity to do Free Voluntary Reading and those behind in reading have to do more worksheet pages and exercises. This practice does nothing but further the gap between weaker and stronger readers. It may also damage the poor readers' self-esteem.

Stephen Krashen was the keynote speaker at the ECIS ESL & MT conference in Rome, 2005. His arguments for Free Voluntary Reading convinced many of the ESL and mother-tongue teachers present. Several returned to their schools and successfully convinced their administrators to introduce a Free Voluntary Reading time into their school's timetable. These teachers report successful results and also how much their students enjoy this time set aside for them to read. One ESL teacher, however, sent me an email describing how an English teacher at her school introduced Free Voluntary Reading:

> . . . she gave the children five minutes for Free Voluntary Reading each lesson. My ESL children complained that it wasn't enough time and also that during the five minutes, when they were supposed to be reading quietly, their teacher talked to them for the whole time.

This example demonstrates that planning and understanding of the rationale behind Free Voluntary Reading need to be in place before it is introduced. Both teacher and child need to understand the 'why' of it.

Teachers interested in introducing Free Voluntary Reading are encouraged to read

Krashen's book *The Power of Reading* (2004). They will find a host of ideas to help them implement Free Voluntary Reading into their programmes. ESL teachers could also give workshops for mainstream teachers informing them of the principles. Parents too would benefit from a workshop or discussion that makes them aware of the potential that developing a love of reading can open up for their child.

Establishing a love of reading is important. However, children also need to be explicitly taught how to read in order to deal with the very different tasks required of them by different subjects. We read a novel for relaxation and fun in a very different way from the way we read a piece of literature in order to write a literary criticism of it. This is different again from the way we read a newspaper to find out what's on at the cinema or the way we read a reference book when we need to research a topic. ESL children need to be explicitly taught how our reasons for reading determine the reading strategies we use. They need to practice the skills of skimming and scanning and interpreting the meanings of words from contexts.

Reading skills, just like writing skills, need to be developed across the whole curriculum. As mentioned previously, texts from different subject areas have different features both in the language they use and in the way the text is constructed. It is for this reason that the teaching of reading cannot be left to the English or ESL teacher only. Teaching children how to read in the context of a subject helps them to understand that subject better.

Pauline Gibbons in her book *Scaffolding Language – Scaffolding Learning* (2002) provides teachers with a wealth of strategies for teaching reading across the curriculum. She encourages mainstream teachers to build activities into their teaching that focus on three levels: (1) Before Reading; (2) During Reading; and (3) After Reading.

(1)   *Before Reading*: In Before Reading activities teachers set up the context and establish prior knowledge. This is the point where teachers introduce new vocabulary and prepare children for the work ahead.

(2)   *During Reading*: In During Reading activities teachers need to involve students in interacting with the text in order to complete a task. This is the time to encourage students to think through their learning and talk about it.

(3)   *After Reading*: In After Reading activities teachers should use the reading text as a springboard to writing or responding creatively to what they have read. This is the time to question the text and to encourage the children to think critically and relate the reading to their own lives.

When teachers use the teaching of reading in such ways as to cause authentic engagement with the text they promote deeper levels of understanding. The approach outlined above by Gibbons and Ada's theory of 'The Creative Act of Reading' mentioned earlier are both approaches that can be applied to children of all ages and to all subject areas. Reading taught across the curriculum in all subject areas and involving the shared responsibility of all teachers, using an approach that extends rather than hinders the ESL child, is the backbone of effective tuition in International Education.

ESL parents should inform themselves how reading is taught in a school. They should be wary of schools that want to place children in streamed reading classes. It is important to understand a school's approach to literacy. Is it a 'back-to-basics' reading curriculum, limited to the English department or is it an approach that teaches your child to read the word *and* the world? The latter will occur in an International School that strives to include every child in every aspect of the curriculum.

## How to Ensure Academic Success

During an 18-year period Virginia Collier and Wayne Thomas (1997) analysed over two million student records of students learning English as a second language in the United States. Their findings were consistent across all regions of the US, across different language groups (over 100 different first languages were included in the study) and across urban, suburban and rural settings. The study revealed that when high-quality enriched dual language schooling is provided for ESL students, they excel in all aspects of their schooling.

After five to eight years of schooling through English and the student's mother-tongue, they found that bilingually schooled children consistently outperformed second language children who had been schooled only in English. They reported that the amount of formal schooling the child receives in her L1 is the strongest predictor of how rapidly the child will catch up in the L2. This factor is a stronger predictor than socio-economic status or the extent to which the child's parents may or may not speak English:

> Of all the student variables, the most powerful predictor of academic success in second language learning is formal schooling in the first language.
>
> (Collier & Thomas, 1997: 39)

This report has relevance for International Education. Historically, International Schools were developed to serve English speaking families and the English-medium curriculum reflected the perceived needs of such parents. However, the reality of International Schools today is that many serve a large number of host country students as well as professional families working abroad from a variety of linguistic backgrounds.

As Virginia Collier points out in her foreword to *The International Schools Journal Compendium* (2003: 8):

> When the demographics of a school's population include a multilingual student group with small numbers of each language represented, then mother-tongue literacy development for each language group, combined with ESL taught through academic content, may be the best choice for support of non-English-speakers' needs.

The Collier and Thomas (1997) research demonstrates that the curriculum for second language students must address four different dimensions and that English language acquisition on its own is not enough to close the achievement gap between L2 learners of English and L1 mother-tongue English speakers.

They demonstrate these dimensions in their Prism Model. The model encompasses these four dimensions:

- language development;
- cognitive development;
- academic development;
- social cultural processes.

Collier and Thomas suggest that if all of these four dimensions are not part of the curriculum and instruction, then ESL students will have difficulty closing the achievement gap between them and their L1 speaking peers.

*Language development* should occur in and across all the child's languages. International Schools should therefore not think of literacy development as meaning literacy in English only.

*Cognition* is the act or process of coming to know or understand something. Teachers need to help students develop cognition by:

- checking their prior knowledge;
- providing background knowledge if necessary;
- stimulating children to think about their existing knowledge in novel ways;
- encouraging them to make new connections between what they already know and the new contexts presented to them.

All teachers should be aware of the cognitive challenges second language children face such as:

- communication in a second language;
- succeeding in demanding academic settings.

In order to do well, second language learners need to be in language-rich, highly contextualised classrooms where teachers focus on the meaning of language and on actively developing academic language. ESL students need to learn academic content even if they do not have a strong level of English proficiency. If schools wait until children have acquired basic communication skills the ESL children will fall behind their peers academically.

*Academic development*: Collier and Thomas (1997) found that academic knowledge and conceptual development transfer from the first to the second language. As the ESL child progresses through school, the academic work becomes increasingly more demanding. One of the most effective ways to develop the child's academic language is through teaching the child content in both her L1 and English.

*Social cultural processes*: Collier and Thomas (1997) place these at the core of the Prism Model. Social and cultural processes impact on the child's experiences in the home, at school and in the broader society. Collier and Thomas suggest that socio-political and affective factors will strongly influence the child's response to the new language. ESL children need a socio-culturally supportive environment to flourish. Krashen's affective filter portrays how psycho-social challenges, especially anxiety, may inhibit the ESL child's performance in class. An International School's curricular content and instruction should do the following if the ESL child's needs are to be met:

- use a variety of media;
- use a theme-based approach;
- provide student-centred instruction;
- develop students' thinking skills using all the languages of the classroom;
- teach explicitly the terminology of different subject areas;
- develop both content and language objectives in all subject areas.

Second language learners need sheltered instruction to deal successfully with the demands of the mainstream curriculum. The idea of sheltered instruction was introduced by Krashen in the early 1980s. Sheltered instruction

- focuses on grade-level instruction;
- provides instruction that is comprehensible, relevant and motivating;
- explicitly emphasises language and content objectives.

Sheltered instruction is necessary for ESL students as they build linguistic, cognitive, academic and socio-cultural knowledge in English.

Collier and Thomas found that a dual language approach to learning is more effective than the English-only method and that the former promotes long-term academic gains for the ESL child.

## A supportive school environment

Administrators and teachers in International Schools should provide a socio-culturally supportive environment that allows natural language, academic and cognitive development to flourish in both English and the mother-tongue.

Progressive International Schools strive to strengthen the academic, linguistic and cognitive abilities of their students. Enlightened administrators and teachers are informed on the research that supports first and second languages being developed together. They build the teaching of their students' mother-tongues into the mainstream life of the school. They also recognise that language is best acquired through natural and rich oral and written language used across the entire curriculum. Teachers in effective schools use children's first language as a knowledge base to build on and extend. They realise that this accelerates linguistic, cognitive and academic growth. Effective International Schools create a socio-cultural environment that affirms all their students' identities and invite all their parents to participate in the process.

The parents of ESL children are encouraged to search out this kind of school for their child. There is a growing number of effective International Schools. One school that has taken the Collier/Thomas Prism Model and placed it at the heart of the school curriculum is the Vienna International School (VIS). Maurice Carder, head of ESL & MT at VIS, provides a vivid description of how successful the Collier/Thomas Prism model has been in the secondary department of the VIS (Carder, 2007).

International Schools that offer the IB MYP have also made a commitment to developing all of a child's languages. In the *IBO MYP Second Language Acquisition and Mother-Tongue Development Guide for Schools 2004*, great emphasis is placed on developing both the L1 and L2 through curricular content in the MYP. The document cites the research relating to mother-tongue development and maintenance from Cummins and Danesi and described by Baker and Pry Jones (1998) as being particularly significant.

This research indicates that students following a mother-tongue maintenance and development programme receive the following benefits (from IBO, 2004:6):

- They avoid language loss and the resultant negative effects, for example Subtractive Bilingualism (where the development of a second language is detrimental to the development of first language).
- They perform at least as well (often better) as second language students who don't maintain their mother-tongue and are schooled wholly in the second language).
- They retain a positive attitude towards their mother-tongue and cultural background when the school shows acceptance of the mother-tongue language accounting for increased self-esteem and its resultant benefits.

IBO schools are being encouraged by IBO visiting teams to set up mother-tongue programmes. One such school recently posted these congratulatory remarks on its website:

> IBO applauds the International School of Phnom Penh. This Mother-Tongue Programme is superb! ISPP is an excellent example of a school taking the initial steps of implementing mother-tongue programmes.

ESL parents are encouraged to find schools for their children that do their utmost to promote and maintain mother-tongue languages. IBO schools that follow the PYP, MYP and IBD are striving to do this.

There are however other schools that have chosen to develop their own curriculum rather than adopt the IBO approach that are equally effective International Schools. The ISB (mentioned previously) has a manifesto that includes the statement, 'Every teacher, a language teacher'. ISB is a school that only offers the IB at the diploma level. It has a mother-tongue programme in the lower school and offers around 15 mother-tongue languages at IB level. This school had 12 of its teachers trained as tutors for ESL in the Mainstream: an extremely valid staff development course developed in Australia that gives mainstream teachers strategies for working success-fully with second language learners. In this way the ISB has brought ESL expertise to the different subject areas throughout the school. This is a school where collab-oration plays a key role (for more information on their approach to education see page 30). Collaboration exists between parents, teachers and administrators, teachers and teachers, teachers and students, students and students. Behind this is a vision inspired by Kevin Bartlett, the school's head, who believes in International Education and takes it seriously. He is an inspiring administrator who is a regular presenter at International School conferences. He was one of the first International Primary School administrators to promote mother-tongue programmes in International Education. As far back as 1991 he implemented a mother-tongue programme when he was the Head of Vienna International Primary School.

## A Clear Vision

Perhaps the key to finding effective International Education is being able to unlock the school's vision of itself. If parents are able to see a clear vision of what the school means for all of its stakeholders, parents, teachers and administrators and in particular what the school means for the ESL child, then they can decide on its appropriateness. Some International Schools do not have a clear vision of who they are and without this they have great difficulty in delivering an inclusive curriculum that will meet the needs of all their learners.

## Implications

So what are the practical implications of the research discussed in this chapter?

### Implications for parents

- Be aware of the length of time it takes to learn a second language and do not put your child under unnecessary stress.
- The demands of tasks become increasingly more challenging as your child progresses through school. Help comprehension by talking through difficult concepts with your child in your L1.
- A school that does not promote L1 learning may damage your child's cognitive and academic performance.
- ESL children need context-embedded materials to help them understand. Does the school provide this?
- Be supportive; remember it can be quite traumatic for a child not being able to communicate well.
- Do not insist on your child speaking English to or in front of guests, wait until the time and occasion is right and this will happen naturally.
- Maintain and develop your child's L1. Research shows that ESL children are more successful at learning English if their L1 is developed to a high level at least through the elementary years.

- Children who are schooled in two languages until the age of 11 or 12 enjoy cognitive benefits over monolinguals.
- Where possible choose a school that has a good mother-tongue programme in place.
- Literacy is important in both English and your language. Does the school encourage the child to use and build on her L1 literacy skills?
- Read to your child frequently in your language.
- Explain to your child's teacher differences in literacy practices between your home language and English (using a translator if necessary).
- Ask the school or teacher if children can have a time for reading quietly. Find time for this at home too.
- Is the school's vision clear to you?
- Are you convinced the school uses inclusionary practices?
- Choose a school that has a staff development programme for all its teachers so that you can be assured teachers know how to teach second language children.

## Implications for teachers

- Be aware of the length of time needed for second language learners to be able to deal fully with the academic demands of the curriculum.
- Teach language and content together.
- Instruction for ESL children should be cognitively challenging.
- Build critical language awareness into your teaching.
- Remember that two languages working together can improve and further 'understanding'.
- Scaffold your instruction to make it comprehensible for all children, for example, use graphic organisers.
- Encourage children to make associations between languages.
- Do not force beginning ESL children to talk.
- Create a natural learning environment using tasks that promote a natural flow of talk.
- Use hands-on activities.
- Remember children learn best through experiences.
- Give children opportunities for cooperative learning.
- Inform yourself of the most common genres used in your subject area and teach them explicitly to your students.
- Find time for Free Voluntary Reading and make it a regular part of your class.
- Build Before Reading, During Reading and After Reading activities into instruction.
- Explicitly teach the most common school genres.
- Use the children's L1 as a knowledge base to teach from.
- Actively encourage children to use their L1 to make associations.

- Read as much as your can on second language acquisition and mother-tongue development.
- Ask to attend international and subject specific ESL & MT conferences.
- Share your knowledge with parents, administrators and colleagues.

# Chapter 3

# *Third Culture Children*

## Introduction

Mobility in the International School community is an accepted norm. Parents, teachers and students come and go but how often is this concept addressed within the curriculum? In too many International Schools children are expected to deal with transition on their own. First report cards often contain comments on how well children are, or are not, settling into their new environment, but how do International Schools actually help students through this process? And how do schools help the other children, those who don't move on but stay? Some International Schools are beginning to realise that they have a role to play and the responsibility to support their students and families as they adjust to the new school community. There are some International Schools that have programmes that facilitate the arrival and departure of the people in their community. Is this in itself enough?

The aim of this chapter is to give the reader an understanding of the term 'Third Culture Kids' by taking a brief look at the work of Pollock and van Reken, leading authorities in the field of transition and mobility. A range of issues will be explored including:

- the definition of third culture child or global nomad;
- the characteristics common to third culture children;
- the stages of transition that children and their parents experience when moving;
- how mobility affects both children and their parents;
- ways of explaining the process of transition to children;
- suggestions on how both parents and International Schools should help children deal with transition.

The term 'Third Culture Children' is chosen to refer to mobile children in International Schools. This term 'third culture' carries no connotation of a 'lesser culture'. It is simply the term used to describe children who follow their parents into a new society. These children are exposed to the culture of their parents and to the cultures of the various places they have lived in. Pollock (Pollock & van Reken, 2001) describes this amalgamation of the worlds they have known as their 'third culture'.

## Definition of a Third Culture Kid

The term 'Third Culture Kid' was coined by Ruth Useem (1976) who with her husband John began research on mobility in the 1950s. As social scientists from

Michigan University, they travelled to India to study American expatriate families living there. They discovered that these families were not part of the host culture, nor were they part of their home culture; rather, they had developed a 'third culture' with the other expatriate people and had established a lifestyle that was different from both their home and the host culture but it was one they shared in that setting. The Useems called the children who grew up in the third culture 'Third Culture Kids'. In 1976 Ruth Useem studied young adults who returned to the United States to go to university after having lived abroad. She found that they had different characteristics from their US peers and defined the third culture as a generic term to discuss the lifestyle 'created, shared and learned' by those who are from one culture and are in the process of relating to another. She defines Third Culture Kids as 'children who accompany their parents into another society'. This certainly seems an appropriate definition for a large number of children in International Schools.

Pollock and van Reken (2001: 19) describe a Third Culture Kid as follows:

A Third Culture Kid is a person who has spent a significant part of her developmental years outside the parents' culture. The Third Culture Kid builds relationships to all of the cultures, while not having full ownership in any. Although elements from each culture are assimilated into the Third Culture Kid's life experiences, the sense of belonging is in relationship to others of similar background.

Norma McCaig (1992) developed the term 'global nomad' to describe these children. Both terms are now used interchangeably. For the rest of this chapter the term 'Third Culture Children', or TCC, will be used.

## What are the characteristics that TCCs share?

- They are raised in a genuinely cross-cultural world.
- They are raised in a highly mobile world.
- The people around them are constantly coming and going from one country to another.
- Many spend time in cultures whose people are physically different from them.
- Many expect to return to their native land.
- They often lead privileged lifestyles.

The first two characteristics are shared by all TCCs according to Pollock and van Reken (2001). The others vary depending on where and why their families are living outside the home culture. International educators frequently observe that children who have moved internationally more than once:

- have the ability to adapt to new cultures;
- are more open to different points of view;

- are more open to new experiences;
- have more self-confidence.

Here is a personal experience that illustrates the importance of understanding transition:

---

In the spring of 2003 I was asked to write a book review for the *ECIS International Schools Journal* of a recent publication. The book was *New Kid in School* by Debra Rader and Linda Harris Sittig (Rader and Sittig, 2003). As I flicked through the book I realised that I would have to read the work of Pollock and van Reken if I were to do justice to the book in my review. This was my first introduction to Pollock and van Reken's book *Third Culture Kids* (Pollock & van Reken, 2001), although I was familiar with the term TCK. At that moment in my life my two older bilingual children were preparing to go off to university in Britain. Having grown up in Italy, their only trips to an English speaking country had been brief holidays with my family in Ireland. As I read through *Third Culture Kids* and *The New Kid in School* I kept thinking how beneficial it would be for my children and indeed I gave them several chapters to read. Their response was, 'Well, yes, a lot of it is commonsense but it does help you understand'. They followed many of the suggestions in the books such as taking photos of home and treasured items with them. They felt that the tips given and the explanation of the process of transition made their move from living in Italy to the UK easier. I was pleased that I was able to make them aware of the different phases of transition and thus prepare them for what was ahead before they left the safety of home.

---

All parents who are planning to move are encouraged to read *The New Kid in School*. Although it is written for teachers and there are lesson plans and so on, it was written by teachers who have experience of International Education, their aim being to help both children and adults make sense of their experiences and understand the changes they go through when they move. Some of their ideas are summarised below.

## The transition experience

Transition is defined as 'the change or passage from one state or stage to another'. There are many normal transitions in life; they are 'normal' because we know they are coming and have time to prepare for them. Examples are: leaving elementary school for secondary school; leaving secondary school for university (within the same country and culture). TCCs, however, also experience unexpected transitions which can involve changing cultures as well as locations.

International Schools have a responsibility to meet the needs of their mobile populations and teachers should be aware of where their students are in the transition experience in order to accommodate their needs.

The five stages of transition are:

- involvement;
- leaving;
- transition;
- entering;
- reinvolvement.

*Involvement Stage*: In the involvement stage we feel at home in our environment. We have a sense of belonging and we are able to follow the customs and traditions of our community so that we maintain our position as a valued member. This knowledge gives us comfort and security in our lives.

*Leaving Stage*: As soon as we learn about having to relocate we enter the leaving stage. Even if we will not be leaving for 6 months we immediately begin to focus on the future. We begin to 'loosen our emotional ties', no longer investing in our personal relationships and responsibilities in the same way. It is quite common for children to fight with their friends at this stage because it's subconsciously easier to leave someone they dislike. There are many mixed emotions during this stage. We are not sure if we want to go or stay where we are. We can feel excited, sad, lonely and anxious all at the same time. We may even harbour resentment if we have not had much say in the decision to move.

*Transition Stage*: We enter the transition stage as soon as we actually leave the place where we are living and have known as home. This stage is almost invariably a period of chaos, uncertainty and stress. (It can be particularly stressful for children if they haven't managed to visit the new country before their arrival.) We usually become more self-centred and may worry unnecessarily about trivial things or our health. A simple headache can be exaggerated into the fear of it being a symptom of a chronic disease. Problems that are small may be exaggerated too; for example we misplace a favourite book and are convinced we will never find it again. This fear may arise partially from the fact that all the usual places we would look for the book have gone! Parents in this stage may be too busy focusing on their own needs and may forget to dedicate time to their children, for example they may forget the usual bedtime and story routine. This can result in the children wondering what is going on. A functional family can become dysfunctional temporarily causing discomfort to all its members. Both parents and children can experience low self-esteem that comes from not knowing how to fit into the new culture. This stage does not end until we have decided to launch ourselves into the new community. There are some people who may find themselves in this stage throughout their stay in a new place: they withdraw and feel resentful and do not know what to do or how to adapt to the new community. Teachers need to be on guard to help children who withdraw and are resentful. They can do this by making them aware of the process of transition, using stories of children who have moved from one place to another and talking with their class about the characters' feelings and experiences.

*Entering Stage*: This stage begins when we have made the decision that it is time to become part of the new community. We begin to take risks and although we really want to get to know the new people and their ways, we still feel quite vulnerable. We worry about getting things right and are afraid of making fools of ourselves in the new environment. Parents and children who are naturally shy may become more so and those with outgoing personalities may become loud and overbearing. This passes as we gain confidence and begin to adjust to the new life. We go though a period of intense excitement, everything is new and we enjoy this, then we pass through a period of culture shock where we feel confused and disorientated. Finally, we feel adjusted and we begin to fit in better and feel more comfortable in the new place.

*Reinvolvement stage*: In this last stage we finally have a sense of compatibility with the new community. We feel we have a place in it and this makes us feel secure. We are able to focus on the present rather than always reminiscing about the past or hoping for the future.

While it is true that these five stages describe only a general pattern that has many exceptions, many of the International School parents I have talked to can relate the stages to their own, and to their children's lives.

## Understanding transition

Given how mobile the world of education is, knowing and understanding these stages will help all involved in international schooling to plan effectively so that there is continual discussion on the issues of mobility. A teacher who recognises where a child is in the transition process will be more able to support her accordingly. Having older TCCs act as mentors for younger children from the same backgrounds can help alleviate the sense of abandonment a young child may feel upon arrival and help her to learn, in her own language, how the school and the people in it work.

Children in International Schools could explore the experiences and feelings caused by moving and being left behind. Educators could help children develop skills that will enable them deal effectively with the many changes that are involved in the stages of moving and Rader and Sittig's (2003) book provides such help. It is an excellent resource for schools wanting to integrate the theme of transition into their curriculum.

Rader and Sittig use what they call the ADAPT model to describe transition. It is an effective tool for schools that want to teach students about the process of transition. Parents can also use the ADAPT idea to talk to their children in advance of a move.

The word adapt comes from Latin; *adaptare*, and the formation of the word is similar in French, *adapter*; and in Italian, *adattare*; and in Spanish, *adaptar*. However the concept of ADAPT is common to many languages. Rader and Sittig suggest that parents talk to children about the many things they will have to adapt to in the new community such as: new country, new culture, new customs, new language, new school, new neighbourhood, new ways of doing things, new behaviours, new feelings, new climate, new surroundings.

Preparing children for a move by letting them know that things will be different is of crucial importance, as is encouraging them to be open to the new experiences they will encounter. Parents who act positively to the new situation and culture will communicate their positive attitude to the children. It is also important to have an open discussion about why the move has come about. Children who are prepared in advance and involved in discussions will know they are valued members of the family. Children need to feel valued and they need people who know them well enough to be sensitive to their thoughts and feelings. This can pose a problem in the early days in an International School for children of all ages who do not speak English. Where possible International Schools should have a system in place where a native speaker (child or adult) helps to make the child feel at ease. Children need to feel they are being protected and to know that Mum or Dad is around or can be easily contacted especially when children do not know the language.

We have seen from Pollock and van Reken's work that adapting to a new community is a process that involves different stages. Rader and Sittig have developed the ADAPT model to explain these stages to children (see Figure 10).

---

### The ADAPT model

*All* is well (involvement stage)
    ↳ We feel like we belong

*Don't* want to go – or do I? (leaving stage)
    ↳ We have different feelings about the move

*Anything* is possible (transition stage)
    ↳ We have feelings of uncertainty as we leave our home and don't know what to expect

*Perhaps* this isn't so bad (entering stage)
    ↳ We decide to become part of the new community and we begin to feel familiar with the way things work

*This* is OK! (reinvolvement stage)
    ↳ Eventually we feel settled and comfortable in the new place and this is OK!

---

**Figure 10** The ADAPT model
*Source*: Adapted from Rader and Sittig (2003)

Rader and Sittig (2003) go into this in more detail than has been given here and they provide excellent teaching tips for exploring the process. The goal here has been to provide parents with a more detailed outline of the process as described by Pollock and van Reken (2001) using the ADAPT model to show how we can explain it simply to children. Knowing the stages doesn't stop them from happening but it will help children to understand that what they are experiencing happens to everyone who moves from one country to another. It will help them to identify where they are in the process so that the feelings they experience will not be such a big surprise.

## What Parents Can Do

So what can parents do to help their child through transition? The following may help (adapted from Rader & Sittig, 2003).

### Before leaving

- Consider the child's age and level of schooling e.g. uprooting a child in her final year of school is best avoided when possible.
- Try and establish a clear picture of where you are going and what you are going to be doing there, e.g. talk with others who have had similar placements.
- Find out all the educational options that are open to you in the new country e.g. are there schools that teach in your language? Go online and investigate all the International Schools in the area. Try and visit schools (use the criteria in Chapter 6 to help you choose).
- Discover and learn about the new country with your family e.g. go online and search for information, buy books about the area, contact the embassy or consul of your new country and see what information they can provide.
- Be positive about the forthcoming move.
- If your children will go to an International, English-medium School, prepare them for this by letting them take introductory language classes. Make sure that they are fun and that the children enjoy attending them.
- Take language classes in the language of the country you will be going to.
- Teach your children a few phrases in the language of the country.
- Explain transition using the ADAPT model to your children.
- Buy educational books so your children can continue reading and learning in their mother-tongue whilst in the new country.
- Include your children in the decision making as much as possible.
- Talk with your children about any unresolved conflicts they might have, e.g. help them find ways of patching up a fight they have had with a friend before leaving. If they leave after having made peace then they will not worry about the lost friendship when they are in the new location.
- Encourage children to bring favourite toys with them.
- Bring photographs of home and pets with you.
- Find time for all the family to say goodbye to places and people that are important.

## Once you arrive

- Be aware that moving is stressful for everyone in the family and that each family member may respond to moving in a different way.
- Look after yourself. You have your own issues of transition to deal with as well as looking after the others in the family.
- Explore the new location as a family.
- Find time to do the family things you have always done together.
- Be patient and flexible.
- Listen to your children's worries and talk to them about their concerns.
- Talk to your children about the phases of transition.
- Stay in touch with family and friends and encourage your children to send emails, write letters, make phone calls, etc..
- Try to become involved in the new community and encourage your children to invite friends home to play.
- Establish friendships with people who speak your language as well as with people who don't.

## Moving back home or on to another country

- Talk with children about the move, explaining that it will take time to adjust.
- Help children understand they will feel different from their peers for a while.
- Encourage your children to stay in touch with friends made abroad.
- If you are moving to another country, try to link up with other families who have had experience of living abroad.

## What Can International Schools Do?

International Schools should educate all their teachers and administrators on transition and mobility. Schools that send their teachers to ECIS conferences will find an array of topics that address such issues. However, not all International Schools send teachers to such conferences. ECIS has many subject committees. There is a cross cultural committee and teachers can contact the members of the committee at www.ecis.org and ask for help and advice about transition issues. The members of the committee are practising International School teachers with expertise in this area. Unfortunately transitions have not been addressed adequately in many International Schools, yet it is the key to understanding the behaviour patterns of the international mobile community on which International Education depends.

Teachers should address transition education through academic content, i.e. it is a subject that should be written into an International School's curriculum. It is important to constantly look for opportunities to incorporate students' background knowledge and experience into class work in all areas. The materials used in class and work put up in wall displays should reflect the cultures of all the children in the school. Artefacts from all the different cultures of the school community should be displayed, demonstrating that the school values, respects and admires all its cultures.

If teachers and administrators value and respect transition issues then the students will also regard them as important. International Schools should recognise that many of their children and their families are having to adjust to living in another culture and that they may well be suffering from culture shock. This can be particularly difficult for children who do not speak the language of the school or that of the host country.

Teachers can help alleviate some of the stress by:

- Making sure they know how to say the child's name correctly.
- Not insisting on an English-only response.
- Learning words and greetings in the child's mother-tongue and teaching them to the other children in the class too.
- Writing important words and phrases in the inside cover of the child's notebook that she can translate or have translated so they are readily available for use when the child is in a specialist class.
- Recording set survival phrases for the child to listen to and practice saying.
- Modifying class work.
- Establishing clear routines.
- Giving homework that matches the child's linguistic abilities.
- Helping the child to understand the importance of maintaining her mother-tongue language.
- Encouraging the child to participate in after school activities such as sports or music.
- Sharing your personal experiences of mobility.
- Building a sense of community within your classroom.
- Demonstrating a genuine interest in other cultures.
- Using examples of other cultures in your teaching.
- Showcasing individual students: many International Schools choose a child to be 'star of the week' and the child shares her life story and background with peers. It is a good way of involving parents; the child can produce work in her own language and explain it in English with or without help as necessary. Activities such as this raise awareness on the different ways there are of reading and writing whilst at the same time acknowledging the experiences the child has that are unique to her home culture.

    Teachers can encourage students to write about moving to their new country or a short autobiography in their mother-tongue and then find a way to translate this into English. Older bilingual children, parents or teachers can be asked to translate it. Teachers can also use machine translations through Google or Babel Fish. These may provide rather garbled translations but they are good enough to give teachers the gist of what the child is saying. The students can then produce a bilingual book.

- Looking for natural links in the curriculum that can act as a springboard for talking about transition.
- Helping all children to deal with the departure of a class friend by establishing a contact address so they can stay in touch, giving them a project to take with them e.g. asking them to take a photo of their new school and write to the class about it, organising a goodbye party etc.
- Responding to an email or letter sent by a child who has left.

## Conclusion

There are some International Schools whose students are still expected to leave their home language and culture at the school gates. This may not be openly declared but evidence of it is found in schools that superficially value differences, showing off the varieties of cultures in their school only at special events.

All International Schools should strive to build units on transition into their curriculum and involve parents, teachers, students and administrators in the process. Transition is part and parcel of many international students' identities and as such it deserves a place in the syllabus.

## Note

1. For more on producing bilingual books see www.multiliteracies.ca or the Dual Language Showcase at http://thornwood.peelschools.org. The Dual Language Showcase was developed by six primary grade and ESL teachers from Thornwood Public School in Toronto working in partnership with York University and Ontario Institute for Studies in Education at the University of Toronto. It is an excellent source of dual language books written by children and is particularly useful for new ESL students in their first few weeks of school.

# Chapter 4

# ESL Parents – Seen But Not Heard

## Introduction

A visit to any International School's Family Day, May Fair, Sport's Day or International Food Day will give the impression of Internationalism. An array of the vibrant colours of traditional dress can be seen behind tables laden with exotic foods that have been prepared with pride and care.

On occasions like these the parents of second language learners are very much in evidence. They are the people beautifully dressed, looking colourful and different, serving their home-baked delicacies. International Schools are justifiably showing off their internationalism and diversity. There will be jean-clad parents from Anglo/American backgrounds serving hamburgers; these parents do not always stand out as different. They may be a minority in numbers in the school but they often set the norm. These parents are not pulled out of the closet for special occasions. They are always in school and they are involved in many of the decision making processes. These parents have a voice and a say in their children's education. In many International Schools many ESL parents do not have a voice.

The aim of this chapter is to look at the reasons why ESL children and their parents are sometimes overlooked in the formulation of policies and curriculum in many International Schools.

The dominance of an Anglo/American culture group within International Schools can be a cause for concern. Such a group may make inappropriate decisions for ESL learners. Some of the ways this dominant culture may manifest itself are described.

Other sections focus on the need for a *culturally inclusive curriculum*. What this means is presented and ways to achieve it are suggested.

The chapter concludes with a list of practical ideas aimed at helping ESL parents to have a say and become partners in their children's education with a school that values their contributions.

## Factors Inhibiting ESL Parent Involvement

There are many practical reasons that impede ESL parents from participating fully in their children's education. For example, it may not be part of their culture to do so. In many cultures the school has absolute power over the education of its students and does not invite or welcome parental involvement. Parents are responsible for the home life of the child. Home and school are separate. I remember a conversation with a parent from Pakistan in which he gave me permission to slap his child just as a teacher would in his country. 'What things go on in school is teacher and school responsibility. What happens

76

at home is for me and Ali's mother', he said. It took a lot of persuasion to get these parents involved in Ali's school life. They did not see the importance of teaching Ali to read in Urdu, believing this could be easily accomplished on their return to Pakistan.

ESL parents may not feel at ease communicating in English or the host country language and therefore feel they have little to offer by being on committees or participating in the PTA. Some schools do make an effort to recruit ESL parents onto committees because they value their opinions as much as they value those of parents from the Anglo/American group. However this cannot be said for the vast majority of schools, who tend to call on the ESL parents only when they are in need of the exotic cuisine and dress that these parents will gladly offer.

In International Education it is important that *all* 'parents are partners' (Cummins, 2004) with the school in their children's education. Second language parents need to be told this by international educators and have the rationale explained to them.

## The Culturally Inclusive Curriculum

International Schools need to implement a culturally inclusive curriculum. Deborah Burke (1998) describes this well: 'A curriculum can be described as inclusive when everything that happens in that school reflects and responds to the experiences, needs, rights and contributions of all learners.' According to this, the curriculum in an International School should be built on 'Who we are' as members of the school community and 'What our needs are': multiculturalism should be evident throughout the curriculum (Gallagher, 2002). A key factor of this is the acceptance and respect for other languages and cultures. The curriculum should address racism at every grade level. International Schools have to find a way of promoting languages and cultures everyday: the International Food Event is not enough. The starting point in implementing a culturally inclusive curriculum is to involve all members of the school's community in the life of the school so as to acknowledge value and include in the school's curriculum the experiences, knowledge and needs of all its learners.

## Dominant Culture – Dominated Cultures

Professor Jim Cummins is a noted world authority on second language issues. In his book, *Language, Power and Pedagogy* (2004) he suggests that, although millions of dollars have been spent in North America on bilingual programmes, teaching assistants, remedial teachers and the like, the proportion of second language children from Mexican and Puerto Rican backgrounds who are failing in schools has not changed despite the costly reforms. He stresses that the reason for this is that the relationships between teachers and students, and schools and communities, have remained unchanged: 'Students who are empowered by their school experiences develop the ability and confidence to succeed academically' (Cummins, 2001a: 179).

Cummins describes schools in North America as having a *dominant* culture and a *dominated* group made up of the many lesser important (as society views them) cultures (for more on this see Chapter 2). Parallels can be drawn between this notion and what happens in many International Schools where the curriculum often meets the needs of the dominant American/Anglo culture and does not take into account the many other languages and cultures present in the school. When schools involve parents in their children's education Cummins says the parents develop a sense of affirmation that communicates itself to the children with positive academic consequences, i.e. they do better in school.

This has powerful implications for educators in International Schools. It means that schools should actively involve second language parents in all aspects of school life. This starts with making all parents feel welcome and taking the time to find out relevant information about the learners' academic and cultural backgrounds. ESL parents should be as involved to the same extent as any other parents in the formulation of school policies. This may mean that the school has to take special measures to accommodate them, i.e. providing translators or interpreters when necessary. International Schools have an ethical duty to keep all parents informed in matters relating to their children. In order to do this more effectively school newsletters, forms, etc. should be written in a range of the community languages and interpreters should be provided at school meetings thus encouraging the participation of all parents in the life of the school. There are International Schools that do make an effort to involve ESL parents but there are also a great many that do not. I would encourage parents to look for the former when choosing an International School (for more on this see Chapter 6).

## How the dominant culture manifests itself

ESL parents need to be involved in decision making processes. Parents can form one of the most important decision making groups in a school. If there are no ESL parents involved then the right decisions may not be made about how ESL is considered. One example is the practice in many International Schools of charging parents for ESL lessons over and above tuition fees. Where this happens it implies that such lessons are outside what the school considers to be normal. Can a school that classifies itself as 'international' really consider ESL students as being outside the norm? In the box below a colleague describes how charging for ESL happened at her school:

> After a presentation at a ECIS general conference, a young woman came up to me. She was a Primary 2 teacher in an International School that follows the British National Curriculum. The teacher was new to International Education and thus was not used to working with second language learners. After the first two weeks in her new job she made a list of the children who were weak in maths or English and gave it to her head of school. Within a couple of days those needing help in maths were receiving it. She didn't hear anything about the group who were weak in English until parents came to her asking, 'Does my child really need this extra English? Can I help him myself? I can't really afford the 30 Euro an hour for this help, on top of the fees I pay.' The young teacher didn't know what to say.

ESL is an integral part of an International School. It is not a token subject. It is not an after-school activity. It is not something we should ask parents to pay extra for. Any school that charges more for it would appear to be indicating that it is not after all an International School. This kind of practice is evidence of the dominant Anglo/ American group exercising its cultural power over the dominated language groups. The dominant group thinks something along these lines, 'you come into our school, not knowing our language and this is your fault therefore you have to pay more until you have learned to be more like us.' In schools where this kind of thing happens it is obvious that ESL parents have no voice. Paying extra fees suggests that something is not right about the child and it has to be fixed in order to be able to deal with the curriculum. This can put a psychological burden on the child and a financial one on the family. If ESL parents are heard in an International School they can say 'no' to the payment of extra fees and voice the opinion that all students should be valued equally in an International School.

Another way that the dominant culture manifests its power in many International Schools is through an 'English-only' policy. This means that a decision has been made that the only language to be spoken in the classroom and sometimes even in the school playground is English. Parents of second language children may even be asked to speak in English rather than their native language with their children at home. This kind of policy has usually been made by some well-intentioned but misinformed member of the dominant culture group who really believes that by insisting on English they are keeping standards high and helping children achieve more. Nothing could be further from the truth. It is the ethical duty of everyone involved in International Education to support the development of their students' mother-tongues (for more on the importance of mother-tongue development and maintenance see Chapter 2). Where this sort of policy exists in an International School ESL parents need to raise their voices and oppose it. They need to ask schools to provide mother-tongue classes for their children and where this is not possible they must at least insist on tolerance and respect for their languages and cultures and this can only happen when the administration of a school, the teachers, the students and the school community as a whole are open to the use of other languages.

If the curriculum reflects only the vision and needs of the dominant group, the dominated group will suffer. The curriculum must have a collective vision of the needs of the community and this can only happen when everyone in the community is involved in assessing what its needs are. If we take a close look at the left-hand column in Table 1, the *dominant group*, we can see that those in control are people who do not speak languages other than English. At many International School conferences an overwhelming number of ESL teachers describe their school administrators and decision makers as rigidly monolingual and uninformed on second language issues. If such a group as described in the left-hand column is allowed to have control in an International School, the decisions that are made may have detrimental effects on the children who speak languages other than English. Those in the central column of Table 1, the *dominated group*, are the ones who are likely to suffer.

**Table 1**  Dominance vs. collaboration

| Dominant group (those having control) | Dominated group (those controlled) | Abolition of groups through a shared vision, shared responsibility and an overriding collaborative ethos |
|---|---|---|
| • Board of governors consisting largely of people from Anglo/American cultures<br>• Monolingual administrators from Anglo/American cultures<br>• Administrators who are uninformed about benefits of bilingualism and matters relating to language acquisition<br>• Monolingual teachers from Anglo/American cultures<br>• Teachers who are uninformed and not even interested in hearing about the benefits of bilingualism and matters relating to language acquisition<br>• Monolingual students from Anglo/American cultures<br>• Students who are uninformed about the benefits of bilingualism and matters relating to language acquisition<br>• Monolingual parents from Anglo/American cultures<br>• Parents who are uninformed about the benefits of bilingualism and matters relating to language acquisition<br><br>⇩<br><br>*Respect for sameness*<br><br>*Language viewed by all as a problem*<br><br>*English seen as the most important language* | • Teachers who do not challenge the *status quo*<br>• Teachers and other staff who are not part of the Anglo/American culture<br>• Parents who are not part of the Anglo/American culture<br>• Students who are not part of the Anglo/American culture<br>• Parents who speak little or no English<br>• Students who speak little or no English<br><br>⇩<br><br>*Parents and students often view their language as a problem*<br><br>*Students assimilate the Anglo/ American culture at the expense of their own*<br><br>*Teachers blindly accept the ethos created by uninformed administrators* | • Board of governors consisting of people who speak English and languages other than English, administrative staff, teachers, parents – including ESL parents<br>• Bilingual administrators<br>• Informed administrators<br>• Teachers who speak out about the rights of children in their care<br>• Teachers who speak other languages<br>• Teachers from a wide variety of cultures<br>• Teachers, parents and students who are informed on the benefits of bilingualism and matters relating to language acquisition<br>• Teachers and administrators who respect the rights of children in their care<br><br>⇩<br><br>*Respect for diversity*<br><br>*Language viewed by all as a resource*<br><br>*All languages have equal rights in the community* |

I came across an example of this at an ESL & MT conference when a colleague shared this story about her school with participants:

> At a meeting held between administrators and parents of children who were leaving the elementary school to go into the secondary section, the head of school, a monolingual, told the parents present that they must speak as much English as possible with their children. They should even speak English at home rather than their own language and encourage them to read only English if they want their children to learn English.

This kind of misinformation is what is disseminated in schools where administrators who are often monolingual English speakers and uninformed on second language acquisition hold the control. Parents who listen to and follow such advice risk their children becoming Subtractive Bilinguals, i.e. English could replace their own language if parents do not continue to develop and maintain the home language. Parents and children communicate better in their mother-tongue: it is natural for them to communicate in this mode. What this unenlightened administrator is suggesting could cause a breakdown in communication both within the immediate and extended family circle. Furthermore, parents whose first language is not English may not have sufficient fluency to be good role models in this language. Yet, another thing that this administrator is obviously not aware of is that the stronger one's mother-tongue, the more cognitive power an individual has in learning additional languages. This administrator shows no awareness that the children in her care may need their mother-tongue when they return to their home countries. She does not see how sad it would be for these children to return to their cultures and countries to live and not be able to read the newspapers, put their thoughts and opinions in writing and perhaps not be able to fully understand legal documents before signing them. English, by this administrator, is seen as being all-important and this view can have detrimental effects on the well being of both ESL parents and children.

In effective International Schools on the other hand, administrators, informed about the benefits of Additive Bilingualism, do all within their power to promote the learning of their students' mother-tongues, both at home and in school.

### A shared, inclusive vision

In the third column of Table 1 is a vision for inclusion of all groups. It is of paramount importance that the key decision makers are people who speak more than one language and that everyone in the community is informed on language issues and the benefits of bilingualism. I'm not suggesting that administrators and teachers should all be polyglots but they should, however, be open to other languages and have acquired at least a working knowledge of the host languages of the schools where they have worked.

If International Schools are to become places where children, as Cummins (2000) says, are able to negotiate their own identities then schools need to stop imposing their authority through addressing only the needs of the dominant group and instead seek to collaboratively involve all group members in redefining their roles and the type of structures that are needed for an International School to be inclusive of all its cultures. As David Corson (2001) suggests, policy cannot be handed down from above; it should come from the community itself responding to its members' expressed interests and values.

### Dominant/dominated: An exaggeration?

Some may argue that there is no need for a discussion on dominated and dominant groups in International Education and that these terms should remain attached to the groups originally described: majority and minority language groups in North America. It is true that in International Schools there are few students who come from lower socio-economic backgrounds and many ESL parents are professional people with a knowledge of languages other than their own who have high expectations for their children. However, it remains important to highlight that second language parents, even though often highly educated, do not speak up in the International School context. Regardless of what might be written in lofty language in many International Schools' mission statements about nurturing global citizens, what these parents and students think is seldom heard or taken seriously. There is all too often a prevailing national identity that they are expected to assimilate and decisions are made by a ruling group of monolinguals who dominate.

Those who do not have a say are, as a result, dominated by practices and beliefs that keep both these parents and their children in positions of powerlessness within the International School context.

### Truly International

There may be no schools that fully embody Internationalism but there are some schools that try and others that don't. Why is it that many International Schools hang onto national identities, i.e. *The British School of* . . . , or *The International School of* . . . that follows an American curriculum? This may simply be a marketing ploy to make them different from the next International School and also to attract fellow nationals (see Gallagher, 2003).

Schools that offer, or strive to give, an international curriculum the whole way through, i.e. the IBO's PYP, MYP and IBDD and also the IPC, prepare children with an openness and respect for cultural diversity that no curriculum steeped in national traditions is able to match (for more on the different international curricula see chapter 1). These are by no means the perfect programmes we should all be striving for but they are some of the better things that are happening in International Schools at present. They at least provide a forum for those students and teachers who follow them to discuss their international needs.

What practical things can be done by schools to empower ESL parents and children? A school that really values internationalism will implement a curriculum that has a truly international perspective and a pedagogical approach that develops an open attitude to other cultures.

## What Steps Do Schools Need to Take to Achieve a Culturally Inclusive Curriculum?

### Employ people who are able to speak other languages and who are interested in language in general

Effective International Schools recruit administrators and teachers of different nationalities as well as those who are bilingual or who speak other languages as well as English because ultimately these are the kind of people who understand what learning a language entails and can empathise with the majority of international students and parents. There should be no place in International Education for an individual who 'doesn't like languages', 'can't speak languages' or 'can't learn languages'. This sort of person simply does not belong and does not have the mindset necessary to work in a school where awareness of language is *all*-important (Gallagher, 2005). International parents and students will have difficulty relating to people who think along these lines.

### Develop an international curriculum

International Schools have to move away from simply adjusting national curricula to try to suit their needs. There are some International Schools that are gradually moving towards a curriculum that suits their student body but some show little sign of change.

In order to develop an international curriculum that is tailored to meet the needs of all members of its community, all administrators, all teachers, all parents and all students should ask themselves four basic questions about their school (Gallagher, 2002):

- What does it mean to us that our school is international?
- How does that make us different from other schools?
- How do we view language? Do we see it as a problem or as a resource? (For more on this see Chapter 3.)
- In what ways does our school need to change to better reflect its linguistic and cultural diversity?

When all members of the school community are involved in answering such simple yet fundamental questions as these a sense of identity and ownership is brought to the curriculum. Mobility is part and parcel of International Education. Parents, students and staff come and go much more often than in national systems. Someone in an International School should be responsible for monitoring this flow and when there is a substantial shift in the population these crucial questions about the school's identity need to be asked again and changes, if necessary, made to the curriculum.

In answering the questions it should become very clear that multiculturalism needs to exist throughout the curriculum and the curriculum needs to address racism at every grade level. Colin Baker (2003) warns that multicultural units that are not part of the curriculum could do more harm than good. He says at best they are colourful but superficial and at worst they simply accentuate differences. This would suggest that many International Schools may need to rethink their custom of one-off international events that are not linked to their students' learning.

An international curriculum must espouse empathy with other cultures and a concern for international issues in its students. It carries the responsibility of passing values of tolerance and understanding of differing ideas on to its students. To be able to do this the curriculum has to be dynamic, able to respond to constant movement and change. It cannot be taught as though it were supreme and closed to dispute. A static curriculum written for the school rather than by the school will not be able to encompass all the values of the school's members. International Schools need to send out a strong message of how all the values of its community are of equal importance.

ESL children need to see their values respected in curricula content in order to feel comfortable and confident in the school context. They need to see the relevance of the curriculum to themselves so as to actively participate in the curriculum and experience success in school. Critical thinking skills have been shown to be useful in this respect and should be built into the curriculum. We should train our students to be analytical about what is happening in the world and in their part of the world in particular. International Schools should train their students to question rather than accept what they are being told.

We need to continually search for universal values and make our students aware that as human beings we have moral choices to make. Choosing, for example, between doing nothing or taking action is a theme that can be discussed from early childhood years right through to the senior years (in the appropriate manner). This surely in the world as we know it is one of the most important things to teach children in any school, but International Schools in particular cannot ignore what is happening in the world. International educators have a duty (I believe) to address the tragedies and genocides of our times and not ignore them simply because they are difficult subject matter. This is especially true when these disasters may be happening in the country of origin of someone from the school community. Events such as those in Darfur, Kosovo, and Aids in Africa, must be addressed through curriculum content. International teachers need to be able to demonstrate caring for children both as students and as human beings.

It is by making students aware of the realities of our times and teaching them to question and analyse that we will move towards creating the global citizens that so many International Schools' curriculum documents aspire to.

### Actively promote bilingualism

One of the main goals of International Education should be to promote Additive Bilingualism and Additive Biculturalism. Additive Bilingualism occurs when the child's home language is not replaced but added to another language or languages. Biculturalism is a near native knowledge of two languages and includes the ability to respond effectively to the demands of two cultures. It is now widely agreed amongst experts that maintaining and developing mother-tongue literacy is the way to academic success for second language learners. The mother-tongue issue should be addressed by all schools that accept second language learners. Old-fashioned International Schools should move away from the idea that administrators are the sole decision makers. They need to look at what research says about the mother-tongue issue and ensure that decisions made about it are not simply based on the homespun doctrine of one individual, but are taken by administrators and teachers working collaboratively and reaching out to parents and students for their input. Decisions about ESL and mother-tongue should involve everyone. Such decisions are vital and demonstrate to staff, students and parents that international values are taken seriously.

### Schools that educate and inform the wider school community

Effective International Schools involve administrators, mainstream and subject teachers, ESL teachers, resource teachers, librarians, mother-tongue teachers, students and all its community members in articulating and formulating an inclusive curriculum. An inclusive curriculum extends far beyond the texts and methodologies of an individual classroom. All members of the community must understand how the community works and they must plan together to create a positive climate for all learners.

Collaboration, tolerance and transparency must all be more than the jargon and rhetoric of curriculum documents and become the air one breathes in the corridors of the school permeating everything thus creating an authentic feeling of Internationalism.

## What Practical Things Can ESL Parents Do to Gain Empowerment?

It is important that parents are aware of the power structures that exist in many International Schools and this is one of the areas that this book investigates. *Informed parents can effect change by asking schools to change.* Here are some things parents can do to become more informed and involved in school life.

### Ask about the school's aims

Parents can seek to collaborate with schools by sharing culturally relevant information about their families and by asking to have the school's ethos explained to them. This can be established when parents first come into contact with the person responsible for admissions. If the school shows no interest in cultural information on the family this may well be a sign that your family beliefs and practices may not be respected or may be ignored. You can question this or alternatively look at other schools. Some International Schools are more 'international' than others.

## Ask about the school's mother-tongue policy

Initial contact with the school is also the time to ask about the school's policy on the teaching and maintenance of your child's mother-tongue. If the school discourages you in developing and maintaining your child's mother-tongue you can try to inform them that this view is wrong (see Chapter 2) or continue your search for a more enlightened school. The good news is that most capital cities have several International Schools for you to choose from (see Chapter 6 for things to look for when choosing an International School).

## Join the PTA

One of the most important things that ESL parents can do is to join the PTA. In many English speaking countries parents are encouraged to play a central role in their children's education. They do this by understanding what is happening in school and the gateway to this is often through the PTA. PTA meetings can be arenas for the discussion of topics concerning the curriculum, the quality of school meals, the purchasing of new equipment or the construction of facilities. They can cover a wide range of issues relevant to you and your child. It is important that you participate even if you are not very sure of or confident in your use of English. If this is the case try to attend the meetings with someone who speaks your language or an interpreter. You can ask the school to provide this service for you or to put you in contact with someone who speaks English and your own tongue.

## Ask about home–school communications

Ask the school to send home newsletters and forms in your language. Volunteer to help in doing this if you have the time and are able to. Otherwise contact your embassy and ask if they would be willing to have one of their translators translate school forms and documents. This will require some forward planning on the part of the school but parents who are involved on committees and the PTA get to hear of things when they are still at the planning stage and may then have the time to get things like translations organised for the wider school community. This sharing of information in many languages does much to affirm the international ethos of the school.

## Promote a multilingual environment within the school

If in your school there are information signs in English only, ask the school to provide them in the languages of the school community. If the school says funds are not available try asking embassies or the big companies that International School parents often work for to sponsor such a venture. If this fails suggest that the school's art or computer department takes on such a project.

## Be a community liaison officer

If your English is stronger than that of other parents from your language background in the school community offer to act as a liaison officer for them by keeping them informed of what is happening in the school.

Use your English to tell the school that all parents need to be informed. Tell the school of your willingness to help out as translator/interpreter. The school has an ethical duty to keep all parents informed and should appreciate volunteers who will help them to do this more effectively by overcoming language barriers.

## Be proud of your child's name

Say no to anyone who suggests a name change for your child. Sometimes administrators or teachers may suggest changing your child's name or anglicising it in the belief that this will allow them to integrate better. A child called Lorenzo may become Lawrence; Su-Kyung, Suzie. This is an abuse from the dominant power group and as such you should say no immediately to anyone who suggests such an action. Inform the people concerned how much you value your child's personal identity and teach teachers and administrators how to pronounce your child's name, providing a phonetic writing of it in English where necessary. Your child is more likely to feel at home with what is familiar and is also receiving an important message that her name is of equal value to the names of her classmates. An International School cannot say that it values diversity in its students if it allows practices such as this to take place.

## Examine the school's teaching materials

When you oversee your child doing homework, look closely at the materials and textbooks used. Inform the school immediately if you come across anything that marginalises or belittles your culture and beliefs.

## Provide language support

Help your child by providing mother-tongue support for new concepts. If you have time, volunteer to help out in this way in school. Ask the school to provide opportunities for your child to receive mother-tongue support.

## Be a resource for the school

Make the school aware that you are a valuable resource. Offer to share your skills and experience in the classroom:

- telling bilingual stories;
- giving language lessons;
- doing ethnic arts and crafts activities.

Offer to give some professional development for staff on aspects of your culture/religious background.

Inform teachers of the verbal and visual clues of your culture. It is as important that the school understands the 'messages' from you and your child as it is that you and your child understand the 'messages' from the school.

### Keep informed about the school

Make sure you understand the reason for everything that happens in the school. When you do not understand the purpose of something, ask the school for clarity. The school ought to be accountable for its attitude towards you and your child.

### Promote mother-tongue learning in the school

Ask the school to allow your child to use her home language freely whenever possible. If your child is a young learner ask if it is possible for her to be taught in her first language as the vehicle for instruction for most of the school day / part of the school day (see Chapter 2 for more on this).

Ask the school to recruit people who can tutor your child in her mother-tongue. If this is not possible monitor the situation as best you can to ensure that the school shows full respect for your language and culture, religious values and interests.

### Ask the school to organise language classes

Suggest to the school that it provides parents with English language classes and classes in the host country language of the school.

### Understand the school's approach to ESL

Parents of ESL students need to ask some basic but important questions in International Education (for more questions to ask see Chapter 6):

- Are ESL parents involved in the decision making processes in this school?
- Are financial resources made available for ESL learners? For example, does the school library/classrooms have books in many different languages? Are the materials used throughout the school culturally inclusive and linguistically accessible? Ask the school to purchase culturally inclusive resources.
- Are human resources available to meet the needs of all learners? Are there enough ESL teachers to realistically meet the needs of ESL learners? Does your child receive lessons from a qualified ESL teacher? Speak up and ask the school to provide ESL tuition when it is necessary.
- Are teachers adequately trained to work with ESL learners? Does your child's teacher know how to teach children who are learning through English even though it is not their native language? Suggest at meetings that some of the school's professional development money be spent sensitising staff to the needs of ESL learners.

## Conclusion

If you do not ask you will not receive and this is the way it is in too many International Schools. The ESL population is the silent majority. The more you are involved in the life of the school, the more you will understand and the more your child will understand as well.

Regardless of what is written in many International Schools' philosophies about valuing diversity, there is often an inherent respect for sameness rather than a meaningful respect for diversity. Perhaps you will not have the freedom to be ever-present due to work commitments but you can still speak out and question by informing other parents of your point of view and asking them to speak on your behalf. You can write letters to the school. You can inform embassies and big companies (who are often paying the fees) about the schools that follow true international principles and those that do not.

By being informed and sharing information and knowledge, parents, teachers, students and administrators can bring about change that will benefit the child as an individual and improve the school community as a whole.

Effective International Schools go out of their way to welcome all their parents and to involve them in the life of the school. Classroom doors are wide-open to all cultures and all members of the community. Every parent is seen as a valuable resource that teachers and students can count on to diffuse and extend the international ethos of the school.

## Chapter 5

# *Promoting Other Languages*

## Introduction

One of the main themes in this book has been the importance of mother-tongue language and development. The knowledge of the important impact that this has on both the child's cognitive and second language development is now well established. However, in the context of International Education, many schools have yet to see the relevance of and then capitalise on maintaining children's L1. We have considered some of the reasons for this. One of the main factors that explain why 'English-only' policies are prevalent in International Schools would appear to be a fear of different languages, especially minority languages. This seems to be something of a paradox in schools that call themselves 'international'.

It is beginning to change in some education sectors and teacher education is the key to this innovation. In 2007 the ECIS and University of Cambridge International Examinations (CIE) piloted a course for International School teachers. Teachers who have experience in the field of International Education can do this course and receive the International Teacher Certificate (ITC), qualifying them as exemplary International School teachers. The ITC is the first qualification of its kind. It is valid for a period of five years after which time it may be renewed by demonstrating evidence of continuing professional development through attendance at conferences, taking courses and by keeping a reflective journal. The features of the course are based on the following five ECIS standards:

- education in an international context;
- teaching competencies for the international educator;
- teaching students for whom English is their second language;
- student transition and mobility in International Schools;
- reflective practice – continuing professional development.

However, the ITC is not for beginning International School teachers. It is designed for those who already have teaching experience. This means that all new teachers to International Education will be in the same predicament as those who have come before them.

There are courses such as 'ESL in the Mainstream' that effective International Schools oblige new teachers to follow during their first year at the school. A course such as 'ESL in the Mainstream' will have an impact where there is a management that is open to dialogue and progress through change.

A way forward needs to be found for integrating children's mother-tongue into the daily lives of classrooms. Schools may come up with economic arguments and lack of facilities for not being able to put in place fully fledged mother-tongue programmes. There can however, be no such argument against creating International School classrooms where languages flourish. This should be a common goal of International Education and one that can and should be assessed in all accreditation documents. Evidence of this should be looked for in every subject and age level throughout an International School. It is possible to move well beyond the monolingual classrooms of the past and move into an era of *Interlingual Classrooms*.

## A New Concept for International Education

'Bi' is a prefix that is generally associated with the concept of two. Bilingual can define the speaking of two languages or a text written in two languages. The term 'bilingual classroom' suggests the use of two languages and, in the context of International Education, is often associated with English and the host country language. The term 'multilingual' is commonly understood as meaning the speaking of many languages. In the International School context many students are multilingual. However, often these many languages are used passively and sometimes they are not used at all.

A new concept is needed for International Education, one that will promote Additive Bilingualism and multilingualism in international classrooms. Students and teachers have to consider their classes interlingual. The 'inter' stands for both the international mindedness that is an integral underlying factor in the notion of everyone being open and responsive to learning about other languages, and it also stands for all the international languages of the classroom having a part to play in extending International School children's knowledge about language.

Effective International Schools often strive to prepare children who function in two languages, each at a high level. Few as yet have managed to exploit the great language learning and awareness potential readily available in the context of International School classrooms with children from many different language backgrounds. Teachers and administrators need to distance themselves from the idea that the only way to do things is through an English-only environment that incorporates only token offers of rather low-level classes in the host country and other foreign languages.

There needs to be a mind-shift towards wanting to know more about other languages. Openness to all the languages of the classroom is critical. Teachers need to abandon their fear of the unknown and work collaboratively with parents and students to learn more about the home languages of the children in their classes. Pragmatic teachers may ask when they would ever have time to build this into their already busy day but it does not involve a lot of extra work. It certainly needs to be taken into consideration when teachers do their planning. Teachers need to know the child in front of them. Language surveys are now commonplace in many International Schools. They help to establish the range of languages used and also the circumstances in which they are used. Mainstream teachers need to familiarise themselves with such surveys so as to understand better the language diversity in their classes.

## Direct Method

One of the reasons that teachers and administrators adhere to an English-only rule in the international classroom may stem from a belief in the 'direct method'. This is a method that was used in the early 1980s in language classrooms. It was built on the premise that language was learnt best when only the target language (the second language) was used. However, linguists and language teachers now have a more modern understanding of the importance of a strong foundation of the L1 and how this can be used to further and strengthen the second language. On a merely practical level it may sometimes be more efficient to explain key words and concepts in the L1. This can be done through bilingual teachers (where available) bilingual students, parents, grandparents and peers. Interlingual classrooms have to be places where the doors are wide open and everyone is welcomed. It is important to bear in mind that until ESL parents are genuinely made welcome in International Schools and classrooms little progress can be made.

## Multilingual Competencies

Currently in many International School classrooms there is little focus on how we can build on students' multilingual competencies. Teachers may not know the range of languages of the students in their classrooms and this is often the accepted state of affairs. In some schools students are discouraged from using their L1. In others, they are encouraged to learn their L1 out of school rather than within. By contrast in an interlingual classroom students will learn through their own mother-tongue and learn from all the other mother-tongue languages in the classroom. There will be a focus on different languages as well as English. In his book *Language Maid Plane* (*sic*), Anthony Burgess (1964) suggests that schools need to teach children about languages, rather than simply teaching languages. In other words, before we teach children specific foreign languages, students should engage in an awareness study of all languages. A study of language is introduced in the early years and evolves into children eventually choosing languages they have learnt about and are interested in studying.

Interlingual classrooms promote other languages rather than denying them. A whole school language awareness and appreciation programme could include the following:

- the origins of languages (where they originated from and how they have evolved);
- the study of different language families Afro/Asiatic, Altaic, Dravidian, Indo-European, Sino-Tibetan and so on;
- the study of where in the world the language is spoken (geography);
- the study of the main religions associated with the language (social studies);
- the number of speakers of the language (math-related activities);

- the language per se (children can study the different writing systems present in their classrooms and schools).

As we can see from the above, a language appreciation and awareness programme can stretch across many subject areas of the curriculum. It can help international children to develop a truly interlingual and international perspective of language. Children can see their own language and culture highlighted and taught as a regular school subject whilst, at the same time, extending their knowledge on other cultures and languages. The potential here for actively teaching international understanding and respect for cultural diversity is evident.

It often happens in many International School contexts that:

- literacy refers only to English literacy;
- the cultural knowledge and linguistic abilities that children bring to school are considered of little or no relevance to what they learn in school;
- ESL parents whose English may be poor are sometimes thought of as not being able to contribute anything to their children's literacy because they don't have the skills in English.

On the other hand, in an interlingual classroom:

- ESL students' cultural knowledge experiences and mother-tongue languages are viewed as precious resources for furthering academic growth and participation;
- ESL students participate actively in all academic areas because the teacher and the instruction affirm their identity and allow them to invest their whole person into their learning;
- ESL parents are welcome in the classroom and are considered a valuable resource. They help develop literacy in both English and the home language. They can also offer valuable opportunities for children to learn about other languages.

There is now ample research (Bransford *et al.*, 2000) that suggests that prior knowledge and experience should be used as a foundation for all learning. Those schools that ask children to leave their languages and cultures at the school gate should be aware of the shaky foundations they are trying to build on.

## Dual Language Identity Texts

Jim Cummins has suggested powerful literacy practices that promote students' identities and the knowledge and experiences they bring with them to the classroom (see Garcia *et al.*, 2006). In 2002, Cummins in collaboration with another university researcher, Sarah Cohen, and a classroom teacher, Lisa Leoni, studied how teachers can set up classroom interactions so that ESL students can participate academically and use all of their cognitive resources to gain access to the curriculum. The collaboration was part of a Canada-wide project entitled, 'From Literacy to Multiliteracies: Designing Learning Environments for Knowledge Generation within the New Economy' and is described by Early *et al.* (2002). The researchers started from the premise that the traditional teaching of academic textual literacy that most schools pursue is no longer functional in the light of rapidly changing economic and social realities. They considered how teachers can teach for cross-language transfer and literacy in a class made up of students from many different language backgrounds even when the teacher does not know any of the languages.

One approach that they came up with was the creation of dual language identity texts. Students were involved in using both their languages to write personal or collaborative books. The children's cultural and linguistic knowledge was constantly brought into the literacy practices of the classroom. The teacher involved believes that students' identities play a central role in their learning. In her own words: 'The way I see it everything has to relate to the identity of the students; children have to see themselves in every aspect of their work at school.' This view confirms what the Collier and Thomas (1997) research proposes and also Cummins' (2004) argument for identity negotiation and identity investment.

In the project the teacher describes how she and three of her students created a dual language text in Urdu and English. The text was a writing project based on the theme of migration that the children were studying as part of their social studies course. The text was written to be shared with children who spoke Urdu in the lower grades and was based on the children's own experiences. The book was called *The New Country*. It was translated into English and Urdu and it was a collaboration between four children. The study documents how the children were fully involved in the creation of the text and how parents become involved to help with translation.

Cummins describes (see Early *et al.*, 2002) the excitement of one of the children, Kanta, who was so proud to show she could write in Urdu. It was such a contrast to when she had first arrived at the school and had been given a pack of crayons and a colouring book by her classroom teacher to keep her occupied while other children were writing in English. Kanta said *The New Country* written in Urdu made her feel proud because it gave her the opportunity to show the world she was capable of more than just colouring. In her own words: 'I'm not just a colouring person – I can show that I am something.' Kanta also reveals the delight of her parents when she went home and told them that the teacher was asking her to do something in Urdu. They immediately became involved in a way that had not been possible before.

Madiha, another child involved in the project, describes how she likes writing in Urdu because 'the Urdu people can understand and also so that my mom can read my book because she doesn't understand English, so I write in Urdu so she can understand it too'.

From a teacher's (Lisa's) perspective, she explains how the dual language text made it clear to her that children use their first language to help them make sense, not only of grammatical structures and vocabulary, but also of the world around them. In her words 'opportunities like writing a dual language book bring out the inner voice of students and make visible to the teacher what is usually invisible'. Lisa reports that the three girls involved in writing the book became more interested and confident at school. Their parents became co-educators in their children's learning and the work that went home was shared with cousins, aunts and younger siblings. 'It was a family approach to literacy'.[1]

Enlightened ESL teachers have taken up using this approach to literacy in International Schools. However, often it is not an approach that is valued and respected outside the ESL classroom. This approach belongs in an interlingual classroom where the teacher understands the importance of prior knowledge and experience and uses them as a valuable source for learning and transferring skills across languages. This kind of instruction communicates respect for students' language and culture and allows them to invest their full identity in the learning process.

## Poplin and Weeres Study

Poplin and Weeres (1992) compiled a study based on 24,000 pages of interviews, essays, drawings, journal entries and notes from four multicultural schools in California. One student summed up his despair: 'This place hurts my spirit.' Beginner ESL children placed in English-only mainstream classrooms where they hear and see only a language they don't understand and are not able to ask for help may well say this International School 'hurts my spirit'.

The students in the Poplin and Weeres study complained about:

- being ignored in the classroom;
- not being cared for;
- receiving negative treatment.

ESL children sometimes have these same complaints about mainstream classrooms in International Education when the teacher doesn't know how to make her subject comprehensible for the ESL child or when there is not enough ESL support in the school.

Teachers involved in the Poplin and Weeres study reported that their best experiences were when they connected with the students and were able to help them. But they said they often didn't know how to help the students and felt that they did not get enough support from their administrators. This echoes laments often heard in International Education.

## Incorporating Students' Languages and Cultures into Learning

In his book *Negotiating Identities* Jim Cummins (2001b) states that prior to the 1970s it was very common in North America to reprimand bilingual students for speaking their home language. In 2007 in International Schools this is still happening. At the CIS conference in Nice 2006, several participants told of situations where students in their schools were being punished for using their first language in school. One teacher recounted how in her school older students were encouraged to report younger children found using their L1 in the playground.

Another colleague reported that, in her school, seniors were being asked to write their yearbook goodbye tribute in English. (The yearbook is produced annually by some schools and records major events of the school year. Senior students in their final year pay to take a page in this book and write about their time at the school and pay tribute to parents, teachers and friends.) In this particular school, the head (a monolingual) decided that, if another language was used in the tribute, then he would require an English translation of what was being said so he could assess its suitability! This head of school, far from allowing students to affirm their identities, seemed to be actively trying to suppress them.

The following is an email I received from an ESL teacher who works in an International School:

---

I would like to tell you about my experiences as an ESL student in America.

Although I was born and raised in Washington DC, my first language was Italian. The memories I have about learning English are very, very negative and the experiences I had were at times traumatizing. This was due to the fact that ESL education did not exist in the 1960s. Teachers were not trained about second language acquisition. Education has progressed since then and a growing number of teachers in State systems are more aware of the importance of the child's first language for second language development.

Is this the case in private International Schools?

When I hear teachers in our school screaming at children to 'Speak English!' it triggers such anxiety and fear in me. I remember how I felt as a child being told those exact same words. The humiliation and fear I felt when I wasn't able to tell my teacher in English that I needed to use the bathroom and ended up urinating on myself at circle time still haunts me today. My brothers and I were regularly punished for speaking Italian in the playground. What message are we sending students when we do this?

We want our students to take advantage of the fact that we speak English at school. But I personally feel that to punish or reward students on the basis of the amount of English being spoken is wrong. It's a negative approach to learning another language. On top of that it is saying that speaking your home language is 'bad'.

I became an ESL teacher because of my negative experience in school. I want to make sure students feel secure and happy about learning a second language. And I want them to feel positive about speaking their home language.

L. Lo Bianco

---

When students' identities are affirmed and extended, they make more effort to participate actively in instruction and go on to succeed. We therefore need to be continually trying to incorporate our students' language and culture into instruction. We need to provide ample opportunities for students to express themselves and their developing identities.

**Figure 11**  A display board written in all the school's languages sends out a powerful message of welcome

There is nothing very novel about a board with welcome written in many languages (see Figure 11) but we should not underestimate its value in saying to the whole community that we are a school made up of diverse languages and cultures.

One of the things that I have tried to build into my work with ESL children is making them proud of what they can do in their own language as well as in English. I frequently invite homeroom classes to come and see what we are doing in the ESL room. This involves the ESL children showing off dual language texts or what Cummins calls identity texts (see Figures 12 and 13).

Having ESL children present in this way demonstrates to the other children just how much the ESL child can do and emphasises their 'funds of knowledge', that is, the knowledge skills and experiences they have that may well even outstrip those of their peers and teachers. They might have knowledge of other language systems and maybe even a broader personal knowledge of the world gained through travel and experience. Our Grade 3 curriculum requires that children write an information report on animals (see Figure 14). With beginner ESL children I read many simple information reports on animals and then the children write their own animal books. The children often do the pre-writing activities in their mother-tongue. They write an 'about the author' page in their L1. They write several texts in English but the animal's name (the title) is written in both English and their L1. The last piece of writing in the book is an information report on their favourite animal done in their mother-tongue and translated into English. When the project is finished the children practise presenting their work to each other and then we invite their teachers and friends to come to the ESL room and see the final product.

For many years I have been doing a pen pal exchange with an ESL teacher from

**Figure 12** Young second language authors proudly showing off their dual language identity texts

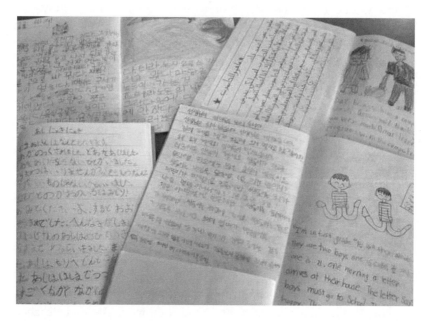

**Figure 13** Identity texts written by 7 and 8 year olds in Arabic, Korean, Japanese and English

**Figure 14**  A ten-year-old ESL child showing his classmates a book he has written on animals using English and Montenegrin (Cyrillic script)

Munich International School. The students write the first letter in their mother-tongue with a translation in English (see Figure 15).

This writing project culminates in the children making a poster about their pen pal. We exhibit these on a display board attaching the letters the children received in many different languages. We then invite the children's homeroom classes to come and see the board.

In Grade 5 I teach in-class with a mainstream teacher colleague. We plan together on a weekly basis. We share the responsibility for this class including the marking of notebooks and general assessment of all students. This is a reading class based on Literature Circles (Daniels, 2002). Literature Circles represent a collaborative learning strategy where children work in groups and each child has a role (job) to fulfil. Roles can include:

- summariser – the student has to summarise the chapter for peers;

**Figure 15** Seven-year-old ESL children reading letters from their pen pals at Munich International School. Their introductory letters are written in their L1 with an English translation

- connector – the student has to make a personal connection with the chapter and share it with her peers;
- questioner – the student has to come up with five questions that will provoke discussion among group members;
- word wizard – the student has to find five new interesting words and share them with peers.

What is good about Literature Circles is that beginner ESL children can be involved in these activities from the beginning. When a child is not able to read the novel on her own the ESL teacher can give the gist of the novel and go over key vocabulary and ideas. The literature jobs can be practised prior to the reading lesson in the ESL room and the students are then more able to participate in the Literature Circle in the mainstream class. It is also increasingly easier for beginner students to find classic texts on the internet and read them also in their mother-tongue.

**Figure 16**  The ESL teacher takes on the role of grammar expert during in-class teaching in a Grade 5 reading class based on literature circles

One of the roles in this class is to listen for repeated errors and then address them on the whiteboard, pointing out similarities and differences between English and other languages where and when possible (see Figure 16). By doing things like this the ESL teacher raises her status: she is not just the nice lady who takes ESL children to the classroom at the end of the corridor, she is a teacher like all the others in the school, someone with knowledge to share.

In conjunction with the global awareness activities at school, the ESL children in my classes discussed the causes of hunger in our world. They wrote poems and made posters, which we then displayed on a board outside the ESL room. Important slogans and key words such as floods, war, famine and so on are displayed on the board in all the languages of the class (see Figure 17). We invited teachers and classes from the whole school to come and see our board. We asked them to give us their ideas for stopping hunger. The ESL children then wrote a letter to Ban-Ki Moon, the new Secretary General of the UN, sharing with him our ideas for stopping world hunger. Korean children wrote their letter in Korean but also sent with it an English translation.

In another project, the ESL children learnt the technical names and stages of the

**Figure 17**  ESL display board with key vocabulary and concepts written in all of the children's languages

writing process with me in the ESL room. They did this a month before it was to be introduced in the mainstream classroom. They wrote their autobiographies going though the stages of the writing process. They did their pre-writing and initial drafts in their mother-tongue. They made a PowerPoint presentation of the whole process and invited their peers to the ESL room and taught them about the writing process before the class teacher had introduced it (see Figure 18). The ESL children proudly showed their early L1 drafts. They showed their peers how to revise and proofread and they presented their final copies. Some chose to do a dual language text so that they could send it to their extended family. The ESL children shared their expertise and knowledge with their peers. These kinds of activities highlight ESL children and show what they can do when they are allowed to make use of all their languages. All of these projects are connected to what is happening in mainstream classrooms. Enlightened ESL teachers often make use of the L1 to help their students learn English.

The more students learn the more their self-confidence grows but for this to happen we need to show that we respect them and their many experiences and talents and this includes what they are able to do in their L1. An English-only environment does not fully recognise the intellectual and personal talents of ESL children.

**Figure 18** ESL child teaching her homeroom teacher and peers about the writing process in a PowerPoint presentation she prepared in an ESL withdrawal class

Cognitive psychologists (Bransford *et al.*, 2000) say that we learn by integrating new input with our existing cognitive structures or schemata. In other words we need to activate prior knowledge and provide background knowledge where necessary.

Anna Uhl Chamot (1992) sums this up well:

> Nowhere is the role of prior knowledge more important than in second language educational contexts.
>
> Students who can access their prior knowledge through the language and culture most familiar to them can call on a rich array of schemata whereas students who can only use that knowledge they explicitly learnt in the second language are limited in their access.

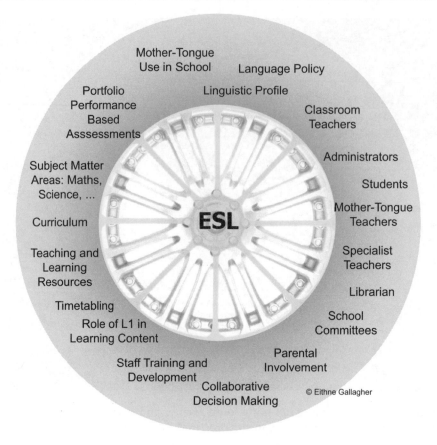

**Figure 19** ESL at the hub of multilingual, multicultural International Education

By activating prior knowledge and background knowledge we increase students' cognitive engagement and enable them to function at a linguistically and intellectually higher level. We also show our students that we value the cultural and linguistic knowledge they bring to the classroom.

## ESL at the Hub of Multilingual, Multicultural International Education

The English-only world that many of us grew up in is disappearing fast. We have to accept the many languages on our planet. International Education has the opportunity to play a leading role in global education by pointing the way forward through promoting an inclusive education for all. This will happen when we stop viewing second language learning as a problem. ESL has to be an integral part of everything that happens in an International School and not something separate.

ESL influences all of the areas shown in Figure 19 and all of these areas have an effect on ESL. Policymakers, the IBO and CIS can have considerable influence here by giving schools strong guidelines that leave no excuse for poor or ill thought out provision for ESL students. Each school community can then plan and work together to make this hub a reality (see Gallagher, 2007).

Interlingual classrooms should become a common feature of International Education. Interlingual classrooms are supportive of biliteracy development. They should be places where educators use teaching as a vehicle to transfer skills and concepts from the L1 to English. The interlingual classroom will:

- have illustrated vocabulary lists exhibiting the many languages of the classroom linked to different areas of the curriculum;
- display translations of students' favourite stories and work;
- contain a classroom library made up of books from many different languages and dual language books;
- have resource books in all the languages of the classroom and bilingual dictionaries;
- instil a genuine ethos of international learning, because everyone (teacher, student, parent and administrator) has something to learn.

It is through this common belief that power will be negotiated and shared and all children will be included in the learning that takes place in classrooms.

Interlingual classrooms can be a place where, through cultural awareness and respect for other languages, the ideas and responsibilities of 'world citizenship' can be nurtured and developed. Interlingual classrooms are places where international mindedness is seen in action. Internationalism is felt and Interlingual children learn who they are in the context of the classroom and the broader society. They learn to work within an international framework of tolerance and respect.

## Note
1. For more on the Literacy to Multiliteracies project see www.multiliteracies.ca. Dual language books can be viewed at http://thornwood.peelschools.org.dual/.

## Chapter 6

# Choosing an Effective International School for Your Child

## Introduction

The 'feel' of Internationalism you get when you visit an International School can tell you a lot more than anything you might read in school documents that quote the number of nationalities present in the school and noble intentions written in mission statements.

Some International Schools are better at moving from mission into action than others. If you as a parent are not able to see any evidence of the lofty ideals written in the school's documents in action then doubts and questions may be raised.

The main aim of this chapter, as the title suggests, is to help parents to choose the best International School they can for their child. Criteria as varied as the following are considered:

- the 'feel' of internationalism;
- the importance of the right kind of assessment;
- the type and organisation of ESL programme;
- class size;
- attitude to native language use;
- exams and tests taken.

Questions to ask prospective schools are suggested and descriptions of what you might find in the many models of International Education are given. Finally, advice to help parents in the selection of a school that cares about Internationalism and the full educational development of ESL children is offered.

## How Can You Feel 'Internationalism'?

As you walk into an International School for the very first time, observe how welcome you are made to feel. Has someone tried to put you and your child at ease? Are your questions welcomed or have you been told that all the answers are in the glossy booklet you have been given? Many International Schools are good at marketing themselves: but don't judge a school by its literature alone. A caring and concerned school will take the time necessary to inform you about the school and to answer all your questions.

### Are all languages valued?

As you walk around the school listen to the language(s) you hear being spoken.

Do you hear only English or are there children and adults freely speaking other languages as well? English may be the language of instruction but if a school requires that children leave their other languages at home then you may conclude that the school will not be supportive of Additive Bilingualism though curriculum documents may claim the contrary.

Look closely at the walls and notice boards. Is there evidence of other languages in use, i.e. bilingual books written by the children, posters advertising school events in many languages, poetry written in various languages with an English translation, projects that are done in two languages? Are classroom displays multilingual or is everything in English only? If the latter is the case, then the school may only really value the use of English and not the other languages of the school community. Are the information signs around the school multilingual or monolingual? Are the information documents you have been given written in English only or is it possible to have them in your language? It is possible for schools to have their more permanent documents written in all the languages of the school and there are International Schools that do this, sending out a powerful message of Internationalism in action.

## Parent–teacher contact

Does the school make an effort to introduce you as a new parent to teachers? Is there time for you to talk to them? Teachers teach best and achieve more in a supportive workplace. Are the teachers heard by the school management? Ask this of both teachers and administrators.

## Promote mother-tongue learning

Does school policy and do individual teachers strive actively to support your home language? Ask them how they do this. Research indicates that competence in English is related to the level of competence in a learner's first language. First language competence is dependent upon the following factors (adapted from Burke, 1998):

- the extent to which the first language is used;
- the level of support for language development that parents are able to provide;
- the level of education the child reached in her homeland;
- whether the language is maintained and developed through language classes in school or by attending after school classes or Saturday school;
- the attitude of the learner and her family to the maintenance of their first language;
- the attitude of the people around them including teachers and their peers in school.

It is important that the school shows an awareness of the importance of maintaining and developing their students' mother-tongues. Some International Schools hold mother-tongue classes during the school day. Others run after school mother-tongue programmes that parents must pay extra for. Many International Schools do not offer mother-tongue classes of any sort. Some even discourage parents from having their child continue with mother-tongue learning. It is important to consider here whether such schools do not offer mother-tongue classes for logistical or financial reasons, or because they do not believe in the importance of students maintaining their mother-tongues. A school or an individual teacher who believes in mother-tongue maintenance can do much to develop the first language without actually sending the child to first language classes. However, a school that does not feel it has an ethical duty to promote the learning of their students' first language, is not likely to be a school where second language learners will succeed.

### School identity

After having spent some time in the school do you have a picture of 'who' the school is, that is:

- Who is the school community?
- Who are the administrators, teachers, parents and students?
- Is there an overall school identity? Is that identity multicultural and multilingual or is it monocultural and monolingual?
- Is International Education really happening?
- Are children learning about world history, world religions, world geography etc. from a world perspective or from a culturally biased one that reflects only the culture of the teacher?
- Is language learning in evidence across the curriculum and in all classrooms? Are there internationalist aims written throughout the curriculum?
- Does the curriculum address global issues?
- Does it teach skills such as collaborative working, appreciating and understanding other viewpoints and conflict resolution?
- When you visited classrooms did you find children interacting amongst themselves as well as with teachers?
- Did both students and teachers appear to be happy?
- Did you get the feeling that teachers are actively committed to Internationalism?

One of the ways you can feel Internationalism is through the teachers' delivery of curriculum content. If a teacher shows a genuine interest in her students she will seek to bring out their knowledge and experiences and use them in the learning situation. If, however, a teacher teaches world history or world religions, for instance, using examples from different countries to demonstrate the superiority of her own cultural identity and beliefs, this is not a person who is committed to internationalism. It is important for parents to both understand and share the school's vision.

### Factors influencing learning outcomes

There are many factors that influence the learning experiences and learning outcomes of children. These include gender, socio-economic factors, parental expectations, physical and intellectual ability, peer pressure, emotional well being and also the maturity level of the child. These elements work closely with other factors linked to the school itself such as teacher–child rapport, teacher expectations, style of teaching, class size, the way the classroom is organised, school structures and organisation, the curriculum and its relevance to the students. All of these things work together to influence self-esteem, motivation and learning.

## Positive attitude towards bilingualism and biculturalism

The attitude of the school to the cultural and linguistic background of its community is of importance to ESL learners whose academic performance depends on the school being able to foster a positive attitude to its pupils. Schools and teachers who want to meet the needs of their second language learners must show them and their parents that the many factors associated with being bilingual and bicultural that they bring with them are understood and valued by the school. If schools and teachers are not able to show this understanding then it will be difficult for ESL children to identify with the school and participate in the learning that takes place there.

## Effective International Schools

There are effective and not so effective International Schools. Effective ones have a clear vision of 'who' they are as a school. They have enlightened leadership and strive to give children the mindsets, values and attitudes that are international. The international ethos of the school pervades all. Do not rely uniquely on the fact that schools have passed accreditations and other inspections. Some International Schools that can declare they have passed such things still fall into the 'not so effective' bracket.

When you walk into a school and can 'feel' its Internationalism then the philosophy statement does not just exist on paper. Parents need to look for schools where they can see and feel the school's international vision in action.

## Questions to Ask a School

The following questions are intended to help parents understand if a school embraces Internationalism and has the necessary qualities for second language children to succeed.

## Questions to ask about the provision of ESL for your child

*How does the school help new arrivals adjust?*

Some International Schools have established programmes where senior students who speak the home language of new ESL children explain to them how the school works. They show them around the campus, introduce them to various teachers, tell them where the bathroom is, how to line up for lunch and so on and then pick them up at the end of the school day to accompany them to where the bus or a parent is waiting to take them home. Often it is the ESL teacher who organises this.

International Schools are becoming more aware of the challenges both children and parents face in dealing with transition. There are some International Schools that have built units on transition into their curriculum. Their aim is to help all members of the community deal with the issues of constant mobility that affect everyone in International Schools. Parents should choose a school that has an established plan for educating children about transition.

*Will my child learn English in a small group situation?*
It is advisable, especially if your child is a beginner in English, that she receives language instruction in an ESL class that has a maximum of eight students. In this way she will receive attention to individual demands and be constantly monitored.

*Does the school withdraw ESL children from mainstream classes?*
There are advantages and disadvantages associated with withdrawing ESL children from mainstream classes. From my own experience and from listening to the experiences of hundreds of ESL teachers at conferences over the last 15 years, withdrawal is necessary and good especially for children in the early phases of language learning. The ESL room or centre can be a safe haven for such children. They will often feel more confident trying out new language and taking risks in a small group that provides a less threatening atmosphere because they are all beginners. The focus of the lesson should not be on language per se, that is not on the teaching of discrete language skills such as grammar and spelling. This is especially true when such skills are taught in isolation from any context, for example the routine use of language work books. It is important that the ESL teacher uses the themes that are being used by the classroom teacher, modifying where necessary, and uses the teaching of this subject as a vehicle for teaching language. In this way the ESL child will not fall too much behind her peers as a result of being withdrawn.

Some school administrators will say that all their teachers are ESL teachers and so immediately push ESL learners into a large class learning situation. This may well work if the classroom teacher is an exceptional, experienced teacher who has had adequate training in how to work with second language learners. However, differentiation (being able to teach to meet the individual needs of all learners) in a class of 20/25 children is asking too much of any teacher on her own with a class made up of multilingual learners with varying degrees of English proficiency or none at all. A team-teaching situation often works well; this is when the class teacher and ESL teacher plan lessons together and teach together, agreeing in advance who is responsible for what. In these types of teaching and learning situations it is much easier for the teachers to create an interactive environment.

The classroom with two teachers present can become paradoxically less teacher-centred. The teachers tend to loosen their control and create opportunities for their students to interact with each other. The teachers' role is to monitor, observe, guide and act as mentors for their learners. In this sort of classroom the ESL teacher is not relegated to the back of the room to give a small group watered down curriculum and less meaningful interaction. The ESL teacher is viewed by the children as being as important as the class teacher. Teachers who team-teach benefit as well: they can learn from each other as they plan together to provide enriching experiences for their learners.

Alexander and Baker (1992) suggest that withdrawal for language classes can amount to segregation and a child's self-esteem suffers as a result of such placements. There has been no research done in this area in the context of International Education. My own experience and that of many second language teachers in International Schools leads me to believe that there is little stigma in International Education associated with being withdrawn for language classes. There appears to be a need for both in-class instruction, such as the team-teaching scenario described earlier, and withdrawal.

To understand this you have only to imagine yourself as an adult going off to live and work in a foreign country without any knowledge of the language. If you have language lessons before you set off at a level you can understand you will find it easier to communicate in the new language once you arrive (even though what you can do will still be minimal) than if you know absolutely nothing of the new language. Withdrawal lessons particularly in the beginning fulfil this purpose in the International School context. They can give a strong foundation to language learning and provide the basic building blocks to which everything else is added. However, the child must not be allowed to fall too far behind with the curriculum as a result of being withdrawn. There needs to be close communication between the ESL teacher and mainstream teacher. The onus is on the ESL teacher to make such classes attractive to all children so that no stigma can be attached to attending them. On several occasions I have had English speaking students ask 'Can I come too?' or 'When do I get to come to ESL class?' and colleagues I have spoken to at conferences report being asked similar questions.

*What subjects will my child have to miss so that she can receive ESL lessons?*

In many International Schools beginner ESL children receive small group instruction at the same time as the English lesson, be it reading or language study, is taking place. This is the ideal time for small group instruction because the language used in the mainstream will be well beyond the capabilities of the beginning language learner and exposure to such lessons is obviously better after the child has some basic knowledge of how English works. In some schools beginning and intermediate language learners may also receive language instruction at the time history is being taught. In such a class the history text may be modified to meet the language needs of the learner whilst at the same time ensuring the main concepts are being taught. This is known as sheltered instruction. For this kind of class to be effective it is essential that it is taught at one grade level and not across grade levels for example Grade 6 only, not a class made up of Grade 6 and grade 7 learners. This is because the content of the history lesson will vary from grade to grade. ESL children should never receive ESL at art, music, computer, library and PE times. These are classes that most children enjoy and they may well interpret being taken out of such lessons as a form of punishment. Multi-sensory lessons based on art, technology and music allow natural language acquisition to take place. It is in the best interests of the ESL child that she participates in these lessons. She will learn by making and doing and interacting with her classmates in a less formal atmosphere.

*If my child is unhappy about going to ESL lessons what advice can the school offer?*

First of all it is important to understand why the child is unhappy. Is it that parents even unintentionally have attached a stigma to such lessons and the child has interpreted that she is not living up to parental expectations? A child may think that she is not 'good' and as a result of being bad at English and has to take lessons to make her better. This can happen if the child was a high achiever at the previous school and now feels that she is not living up to her own internal high expectations. It may be that the class teacher or other children have made the child feel bad about attending ESL classes by singling the child out, calling the classes 'special' English indicating that the child is different and in need of special attention. Sometimes children who transfer from one International School to another may feel they already know English and are no longer in need of ESL instruction. Careful assessment is important here as is a clear explanation to the child of why she is in need of further assistance when this proves to be the case. Generally when children are given reasons for their placement in a programme, they tend to accept them.

It is necessary that the child, parents and teachers understand the rationale of the child's placement for ESL instruction so that the child does not receive contradictory messages as to the validity of such classes. It is important for children with little English to be given a simple explanation and reassurance that the teacher is aware of how much the child knows in her mother-tongue. The teacher needs to let the child know that she is aware that English is not the language the child is used to communicating in but it is the language she needs to learn well in order to succeed in her new school. This should help relieve the child's anxiety. Obviously this message is best delivered in the child's first language. Teachers can also alleviate initial stress by allowing children to write, make mind maps and brainstorm in their mother-tongue until they are able to do these things in English. It is not uncommon for children, particularly those in their early teens, to be unhappy with the family's move. They miss their friends, their everyday routines etc. and as a result go through a period where they refuse to participate in the new school, new culture, new language. Many International Schools have counsellors who are trained to talk to the children on such issues. If the child is still in the early stages of learning English it is advisable that an interpreter is present at such sessions. When a child is unhappy at school, parents and teachers have to work together to find out why and come up with creative and alternative measures to resolve the matter.

*Do the teachers who teach English as a second language have training and qualifications in this subject?*

International Schools should employ teachers who have credentials in ESL. Many do but some do not. Those schools that do not have qualified ESL teachers reason like this: 'if you can speak English you can teach English'. This is certainly not true. In some schools teachers who may not be performing up to standard in a large classroom situation are sometimes asked to teach ESL, the idea being that it is easier to deliver lessons to a small group of learners. These individuals will often have no background in the teaching of English as a second language. This sort of situation when it occurs is unethical and unfortunate for the students. International Schools should employ qualified language teachers who have had training in Applied Linguistics or ESL and are competent in several languages, in other words, people who understand the workings of language.

*How long will my child need ESL lessons?*

There are many factors that influence the length of time it takes to learn a second language. Children demonstrate a wide degree of variation in their rate of second language acquisition. Some factors are:

- the student's motivation and attitude to learning the second language;
- the student's personality and learning style;
- the type of instructional programme;
- how well the child's first language has been developed;
- access to first language speakers of English;
- the status of the child's first language and English.

Jim Cummins (2004) makes a fundamental (if disputed) distinction between conversational and academic proficiency and the length of time it takes to achieve each. He defines these as BICS, and CALP (see Chapter 2). Cummins suggests that it can take two years for ESL learners to acquire the BICS needed to communicate in everyday language and from five to seven years to catch up to their English speaking peers in CALP, that is, the academic language necessary to succeed in school.

Does this suggest that ESL students should stay in ESL programmes for five to seven years? No, not if by ESL programme we mean a withdrawal from the mainstream into classes of children with limited English skills. It is advisable that ESL students who have not yet developed academic language proficiency are monitored and taught by teachers who are informed on second language acquisition.

In an International School every teacher is an ESL teacher. There is no point in the school hiring a fabulous science teacher if she is only able to deliver her subject to monolingual English speaking students. She has to be able to teach all the students in front of her. To ensure that every teacher is an ESL teacher administrators and teachers need to be informed on second language acquisition and trained in second language teaching strategies and techniques. Language must be viewed across the curriculum and everyone must share in its teaching.                              ·

*How is the ESL programme organised?*

There are many approaches to ESL in International Education but the most commonly used are:

- self-contained;
- withdrawal;
- immersion.

Many schools use a combination of these approaches. They are explained in turn here, ending with the mixed approach.

*Self-contained*: Some schools run language centres where they place ESL children in a self-contained learning environment (classes made up of ESL children only) until they feel their command of English is sufficient enough to deal with the language demands of the mainstream classroom. There are schools that adopt this kind of approach for the first two or three weeks of term to teach the children basic survival language i.e. they are taught set phrases such as, 'Can I go to the bathroom please?', 'Can I get a drink please?' Other schools keep ESL children in self-contained environments for two to three months.

*Withdrawal*: In some schools ESL children may initially be withdrawn from the mainstream on a daily basis. If the school has several ESL teachers the children may be taught in levelled classes such as beginner, intermediate and advanced. There are schools that organise these classes according to the grade level i.e. children are taught with children from the same grade level. Other schools group the ESL children based on their English language ability with children from different grade levels. Certain schools withdraw ESL children from mainstream classes for English language lessons only and the focus of these lessons may be on the learning of English grammar. Other schools withdraw ESL children for language classes and for language support in specific subject areas too. Some International Schools provide a programme where children are withdrawn for language classes but also have in-class support from an ESL teacher (i.e. the ESL teacher goes into the classroom to help the child with subjects such as science, geography and history).

*Immersion*: Immersion education is based on the idea that children learn a second language as they do their first, that is to say, subconsciously. In the International Education context this means that most subject content is taught through the second language.

Some International Schools that adopt the immersion approach often place second language children in the mainstream classroom from the very beginning with minimal ESL support. The classroom teacher may or may not have an aide. The child often finds herself in a class of more than 20 children and has to cope as best she can.

Parents should be careful about placing their child in an 'immersion programme' in an International School. Children learning their first language naturally, in the home are not aware they are learning language. Parents simplify their speech when they talk to the child and constantly repeat phrases to ensure the child understands. In a true immersion context teachers use what is known as caretaker speech to emulate the way a parent communicates with her child. Immersion is popular in Canada and the general view there is that the younger the child is when placed in an immersion programme, the better. Teachers who work in immersion programmes in Canada tend to be bilingual and have a background in second language acquisition. This is not the case in many International Schools that claim to have an immersion programme. Often teachers have no training in second language acquisition and therefore do not know how to make what they are teaching comprehensible to children who do not

know English well. Often older children placed in these so-called immersion programmes find themselves submersed in the English language and it's up to the child
to swim – or sink, as the case may be.

*A mixed approach*; Some of the large International Schools at the forefront of International Education employ several ESL teachers and are able to have an ESL teacher
for each grade level in the school. The ESL teacher is responsible for working with
the teachers and students of one grade level only. At the other end of the spectrum
there are large International Schools with large populations of ESL children that may
employ only one ESL teacher per school section, i.e. an ESL teacher for the elementary
and an ESL teacher for the secondary. The fact that International Schools are accredited does not necessarily mean that a school will provide adequate ESL instruction.
Accreditation inspections often go no further than to check that schools make some
sort of provision for the needs of their ESL learners – how they do it, how much they
provide and whether or not there is an extra charge for it is left largely up to the individual school. Choose a school that has a team of qualified ESL teachers that is able to
offer a combination of withdrawal and in-class teaching and that will monitor your
child as she progresses through school.

### What is taught in ESL classes?

What is actually taught in an ESL class depends very much on the kind of programme
that is on offer. Seek out schools that have an ESL department with a coordinator
whose role is to interact with other departments to establish a coherent language
policy and who is an advocate for the needs of second language learners in a whole
school forum. Schools that provide each grade level with an ESL teacher demonstrate
that they take the needs of the ESL children seriously. An ESL teacher who is responsible for one grade level only has the time to maintain good home–school links and to
liaise with the classroom teachers and this ensures that what she is teaching is linked
to the curriculum. A school, on the other hand, that has a large body of ESL students,
one ESL teacher in the elementary and one in the secondary and no ESL coordinator
shows it does not take the needs of its ESL population seriously enough. In such a
school there is not likely to be a whole school vision for the teaching of ESL. The low
staffing levels means that teachers will probably be able to offer only a withdrawal
learning situation. The ESL classes may well have to be made up of students from
different grade levels making it very difficult for the ESL teacher to link her teaching
to the content of the curriculum. The ESL lessons may focus on language without any
ties to what is happening in the child's mainstream classroom. As a result of this the
child may fall behind her peers in academic learning. Ask about the number of ESL
students in the International School and the number of qualified ESL teachers the
school provides.

If a school follows the IB PYP or MYP or the IPC, parents can be assured that there
is an attempt on the part of the school to follow an international vision that includes
adequate provision for ESL learners. However, Terry Haywood (2002: 182) warns
that:

> . . . there is some danger in seeing these programmes as the only legitimate format for international curricula whereas there is no a priori reason to presume that schools cannot identify strategies to develop their own version if managers and leaders perceive that local circumstances call for a different approach.

Some see the IB curriculum as too heavily influenced by British and US curricular organisational models and this is perhaps a legitimate criticism. Such programmes do have a healthy ESL and mother-tongue component created by enlightened leaders and practitioners. The IB MYP produced a guide for schools on second language acquisition and mother-tongue development (IBO, 2004). It is both thorough and relevant. Schools that follow such programmes are more likely to be informed on issues that are pertinent to the needs of ESL learners. There is a risk with those schools that develop their own international curriculum that it may be based on parochial or traditional ideas rather than on current and informed research. Look for an International School that:

- offers an ESL programme that incorporates the teaching of language into the themes being taught in regular classes;
- allows and encourages its students to use their mother-tongue to make real associations with the concepts being taught;
- offers a basic foundation course for beginning ESL students,
- provides ongoing support for ESL learners for as long as they need it.

Do not choose a school where the child's academic learning is put on hold until the school deems the child's English is of a high enough standard to deal with academic subjects. It is important that the content and methodology of the ESL classroom reflects and relates to what is being taught in the mainstream classroom. Also, do not choose a school that places children with little or no ESL support in mainstream classrooms believing that with exposure to English they will acquire the necessary language on their own.

It is an established research finding (e.g. Hopkins *et al.*, 1994) that leadership through heads or principals is a very important contributing factor in creating a school's ethos, identity and ultimately its success or failure as an institution. Parents need to speak with the leaders of the school and discover if they are monolingual and monocultural in outlook or genuinely interested in other languages and cultures. If the latter is the case they are more likely to have the mindset that is needed to lead an International School in developing an internationally minded curriculum that will allow all children of all cultures to be successful in school.

*How does the school know when my child no longer needs ESL lessons?*

Some schools use standardised tests to provide evidence that the child no longer needs ESL lessons, others create their own exit criteria tests. Many schools rely on how the child can perform on the mainstream classroom tests. Standardised tests are objective tests normed on specific populations of students often used in national systems. One such test less commonly used now in International Education is the Iowa Test of Basic Skills. One must question the rationale of International Schools following national or state curricula and using the standardised tests connected to them or worse, using standardised tests while not teaching the curriculum that goes with them. Surely if an International School wants to measure its students it should measure them against other international students. International Schools need to ensure that the assessment instrument is valid for the group of students being assessed.

The Australian Council of Educational Research (ACER), has produced the International Schools Assessment (ISA). This test was created for students from International Schools. It tests children in the areas of reading, writing and maths. It claims a broad cultural base and is a combination of multiple choice and open-ended questions. It requires students to present written responses and use higher order thinking skills. Over 90 International Schools participated in the ISA 2006 assessment. The ISA is a step forwards and an attempt to break away from the cultural bias that is so commonly found in the standardised tests produced for national or state systems. However, even such a test is only of partial value in assessing the ESL child. Decisions, to be reliable, must be based on how the child performs in real classroom activities. Teachers who collect samples of a child's writing over a period of time can learn much more about the real progress a child has made than anything they will learn from one-off testing.

The decision about when a child should stop receiving ESL lessons should be made by the classroom teacher and ESL teacher together and based on observations of how well the child is able to deal with what is happening in the mainstream classroom. In a situation where the classroom teacher and the ESL teacher work closely together and where the classroom teacher is informed on strategies that work with second language learners the transition to the child working independently in the mainstream is smoother than if there is no collaboration between ESL teacher and classroom teacher.

If the ESL teacher does not know what is going on in the mainstream classroom and if the classroom teacher does not know what is going on in ESL lessons, the child will not know either and will have a difficult time making sense of school.

A shared vision is important and it is one of the things parents need to discover about the school. Is there a whole school vision and does everyone in the community share it? Perhaps the simplest way to approach this question is to ask:

- Are all the teachers trained to work with ESL children?
- Who is responsible for my child, the class teacher or the ESL teacher?

If a school does not reply that both the class teacher *and* the ESL teacher are responsible it may imply that there is little or no collaboration between the teachers. In an International School complete beginners in English need both the ESL teacher and the classroom teacher. Both teachers should share responsibility for the child. As the child progresses in English and is more able to deal with the demands of the mainstream curriculum the responsibility will shift.

Effective International School teachers are very aware of their role as language teachers and will do their best to make what they are teaching comprehensible to all their learners. However, there are many constraints for those classroom teachers who may have between 20/25 children to work with. They have a curriculum to teach and they will have in any group children with varying degrees of language competence, children who have specific learning needs, children who have emotional difficulties, and from one day to the next they can have a child arrive with no English whatsoever. This is a typical breakdown of the children who make up an International School classroom.

The job of teacher is a challenging one and an effective teacher will rise to the challenge. However, many teachers have not had adequate training in their preparation on second language issues and thus may be ill prepared to meet the needs of their second language learners who may represent the majority in their classroom. Many schools now offer staff development courses for their mainstream teachers in an effort to inform and give them strategies for working with ESL children. There are also International Schools that do not offer such training and simply leave the inexperienced teacher to get on with the job. Thus the question to ask is whether or not the International School provides training to all its teachers on how to work with ESL children.

*What is the average class size in your school?*

Class size varies in International Schools and there is normally a difference between divisions (elementary and secondary) of acceptable class size. In many schools the heavy legacy of the past still lingers in the approval of very large primary school classes and smaller classes in secondary. There are some schools that have adopted a policy of keeping the class sizes as low as 12 students per teacher. There are many that have large classes but employ aides to help the classroom teacher. This is most common in elementary schools. In many schools there may be 25 students per class teacher. Parents should choose a school that keeps the class size to a maximum of 20 students, especially in the elementary years. The school should be asked if teacher aides are normally employed. It is important however to establish what the role of the aide is and to ensure that teaching is not left to individuals who have not had the necessary training to do the job well.

## Questions to ask about the maintenance and development of your child's mother-tongue

*Does the school think it is important that my child learns her mother-tongue?*

The best answer to this question is 'yes'. Any International School that suggests that for the time being it is more important to focus on English only is wrong. ESL parents must understand that their children will need five years or more to catch up with the performance of native speakers of English in their classes. This time period assumes that an effective programme of ESL support is in place. Research indicates that they are more likely to reach this goal if they can read and write well in their mother-tongues (Cummins, 2004). Any administrator or teacher who tells you, 'just keep speaking your language with your child and she will be all right' is misinformed. Literacy in the mother-tongue contributes significantly to children's overall academic success and is obviously of crucial importance if children return to their countries of origin.

*Is it possible for my child to have language classes in her mother-tongue during the school day?*

Most International Schools provide language lessons in the host country language in the elementary and upper grades. It is uncommon in the early childhood years. A school that says 'yes' to the question above is obviously aware of the importance of the mother-tongue development and is a school that values all of the languages of its community. Several schools have impressive mother-tongue programmes. There is one school that includes 18 mother-tongue classes in its regular elementary school timetable. In another International School it is possible for middle school students to receive mother-tongue classes during the school day but they are paid for by the parents. Not all International School administrators are aware of the benefits that would accrue to their young children if such programmes were implemented. The majority of International Schools that offer mother-tongue programmes do so as an after-school activity and ask the parents to pay the tuition fees.

*What can the school do to help my child maintain her mother-tongue?*

There are International Schools that are informed about local Saturday schools that allow children to continue learning in their language whilst abroad. You will find this kind of school in many capital cities. Ask the school if it has information about Saturday schools for your language. If there is no local Saturday school available for your home language ask the school if it will help you to locate a good mother-tongue teacher for your child. Enquire if the school will let you use one of the classrooms for mother-tongue lessons. Some schools charge for the use of their premises, others do not.

There are International Schools that support mother-tongue learning from kinder-garten to Grade 12. There are some that manage to do this for many of their languages in the school day, others organise classes after school. Most schools ask parents to pay the mother-tongue teachers privately for these lessons. There are schools that attempt to reach out to parents by helping them to find mother-tongue teachers and offer school facilities and administrative support.

After-school programmes may make mother-tongue languages seem to the child as less important than all the lessons that are taught during the school day. They are weighted with the same importance as ballet classes or basketball: demoted to an after-school activity. This is not the message we want to give to international children. The fact these classes are after school may prevent the child from participating in other clubs and activities after school.

Children from the host country language in the vast majority of International Schools benefit from established host country language programmes that are built into the school curriculum and covered by the regular school tuition fees. English language classes and host country classes may therefore be perceived as being more prestigious and worthwhile. Mother-tongue speakers of English and host country speakers learn to read and write their languages as part of the normal school programme. The children from other language backgrounds are lucky if the school is willing to give them space to attend classes in their mother-tongue at the end of the school day.

It may well not be possible to find an International School that fully practises Internationalism where all nationalities are really considered on an equal footing. But surely it is an ideal that is worth striving for? The more a school tries to bring the many languages of its community into the daily learning and life of the school, the more truly it will live up to its international ideals.

Choose a school that shows a genuine interest in other languages by providing your child with classes in her mother-tongue. If this is not possible ascertain that the school understands the importance of mother-tongue development and is willing to help you in whatever way it can to promote your child's learning of her mother-tongue.

There are some governments that give financial support for mother-tongue instruction abroad such as the Swedish and Norwegian governments. Sometimes companies will subsidise language instruction. There are national educational authorities that encourage students to follow distance learning programmes such as the French CNED (Centre National d'Enseignement à Distance). This programme allows French nationals living abroad to sit national exams.

More needs to be done in many International Schools regarding the issue of mother-tongue development and maintenance. Ignoring the research (e.g. Collier & Thomas, 1997) in this important area places students at risk of underachievement and may weaken their cultural and linguistic identity.

### Questions to ask to ensure that your cultural and religious beliefs will be respected by the school

There are secular and religious International Schools. If you choose to send your child to a religious school, even though your family does not practise that school's religion, ascertain if the school has an open attitude to other faiths and if an interfaith dialogue exists in the school. Here are some questions you can put to the school to help understand its approach to religion:

- My child is from a different religious background. Will she be expected to attend religion classes?
- What is organised for children of other faiths at religion time?
- My child needs to learn our religious language to take part in our religious customs, is it possible for her to do this whilst the other children are studying their religions?
- In our religion we practise prayer a number of times a day. Is there a room where

my child can go to pray? Will the school and all the teachers understand my child's absence from class in order to pray?

- Our religious community has special celebrations at certain times of the year, my child will need to be absent from school on these occasions. Is this acceptable in your school?
- For religious reasons my child cannot attend mixed PE classes or swimming lessons. Is this acceptable at your school?
- I do not want my child to participate in religious celebrations at your school. Is this acceptable?
- Can my child wear religious dress to school?

One of the most important decisions for parents is the selection of the right school for their children. Acceptance of different religions is a key element in multiculturalism. In choosing the school that is right for your child you need to discover if the school values the dignity and faiths of all its students.

## Questions to ask on how your child will be assessed as her English develops

International Schools vary greatly in their assessment practices. Some, especially those linked to national or state curricula will use the tests and practices that are associated with them. However, such tests may not always be appropriate to use with children who are still learning the language that the test is given in. Other International Schools have a good understanding of what is appropriate in the testing of second language students and make every effort to assess students using a broad variety of methods.

Here are some questions on child assessment to put to schools. They cover the three areas of:

- initial placement;
- ongoing assessment;
- exit criteria.

*Will my child's English be tested before she is accepted by your school?*

Many International Schools have an open-door policy of accepting ESL children that is not dependent on their level of English. There are, however, some International Schools that will only accept a certain percentage of children from the host country background. They may require that these children have already had some tuition in English and may also stipulate that at least one of the child's parents should be fluent in English. Some International Schools will not accept beginner ESL children into the higher grades on the (rational) grounds that they would not have sufficient time to learn enough English to pass the final exams.

*My child speaks no English whatsoever. Does she still need to take an English test?*

The answer to this should be obvious. If a child knows no English then it is impossible to test her English. Yet, unfortunately, this is still the practice in some International

Schools. At a roundtable on assessment at an ESLMT conference in 2005, a colleague reported an incident that happened in his school:

A new child and his family were interviewed by the admissions officer at the school and a question arose over whether the French-speaking child should be placed in Grade 2 or Grade 3. The admissions person sought guidance from the head of the Elementary who said, 'lets give him a reading and maths test'. The director of admissions, who was quite well informed on language acquisition (being the father of bilingual children himself), suggested that an English and a maths test would be a waste of time as the child spoke no English. The Head insisted if the child wanted to come to this school he had to be tested in English. The learning resource specialist was called on to give a diagnostic reading test to the child. After a few minutes she realised it was a waste of time and asked her colleague the ESL teacher who spoke French to take over. The ESL teacher found a little 7 year old close to tears. She spoke to him in French helping him to relax and did a miscue analysis [see the glossary for an explanation of miscue analysis] of his reading in French and asked him some comprehension questions. She later informed the head that the child was a fluent reader of French and should be placed in an age-appropriate class.

There is no excusing or explaining the ignorance of the administrator who would make such a pointless decision. Placing a 7 year old in such an intimidating situation is also cruel, misguided and uncaring. If a school wants to know about a child's ability to read or write and the child has no knowledge of English then the school must rely on reports from the child's previous school or provide testing in the child's first language. Parents can also be a valuable source of information as to the child's strengths and weaknesses, as can the student. However, such information should perhaps be obtained with the help of an interpreter in the child's early days at the school.

*Will my child have to take a test in maths and other subject areas?*
The most commonly tested areas are reading, writing, speaking and maths. If your child has very little English the maths test should be simply computational, as word problems would not reflect her knowledge of maths but simply highlight her language difficulties. There are some International Schools that still administer IQ tests in an attempt to learn something about the student's ability before admitting her to the school. These tests are normed on the culturally dominant Anglo/American group and should not be administered to ESL students until they have had sufficient time to acquire cognitive and academic language proficiency. If such tests are administered for the purpose of assessing ability, they should be given in the student's mother-tongue.

When a child enters an International School with some English the school has to ascertain what knowledge the child has. Is it enough for her to be placed in the mainstream with or without support? Will the child need extra lessons in English to help her deal with class work? Some International Schools use commercially available placement tests to make such a decision. These tests are often discrete point tests that analyse the language into its smallest units, e.g. a grammatical rule or a phonemic distinction and they assess the learner's knowledge or ability in this area. They involve an unnatural, largely mechanical use of language out of context where the form of the language is more important than the meaning. Many schools use these kinds of tests because they are easy and quick to mark because each test item has only one correct answer. However, schools learn very little about a child's language repertoire from such tests.

Schools that administer tests based on their mainstream programme will gather a more complete picture of what the ESL child is able to do. An example of this is to listen to the child reading from a mainstream text and have them answer comprehension questions or label a diagram based on what they have read. Similarly, in order to evaluate a new student's writing effectively, teachers should engage the student in an oral activity where the context for the writing is established. It is important to provide ESL students with the opportunity to write about something with which they are already familiar. A discussion prior to the writing task to determine what their interests are is necessary and this will also help to put them at ease. Such tasks are common practice in many schools. They provide more information than can be obtained from fill-in-the-blank grammar tests. One thing that must always be remembered in initial placement tests is that the child may not perform well due to fear and test anxiety. However, such fear is relieved when the child is asked to perform a reading or writing task that is somewhat meaningful to her rather than a fill-in-the-blank type of test.

*Will my child be placed with younger children?*

There are some schools that suggest placing the child in a class with younger children in order to give the child more time to learn English. A Korean mother with excellent English told me that she went to live in America when she was 11 years old and was placed with six-year-old, Grade 1 children so she could learn the sounds of the English language. Thankfully this kind of thing doesn't happen any more.

It is advisable to place ESL children in an age-appropriate group. Placing them with younger children may damage their self-esteem and interfere with their linguistic and social development, all of which develop better when they are with children of their own age.

*Are children grouped according to language ability in your school?*

There are International Schools that group children by language ability. In the elementary school this mainly occurs for the teaching of the English language and reading. In the secondary school this streaming of children can occur in some schools for all classes that are considered to have a strong language component i.e. History and English literature.

Children who have little or no knowledge of English should be grouped with children the same age for language classes. In this way the ESL teacher can use the themes and content from the mainstream class for language instruction. An International School that focuses too much on grouping children according to their language ability risks segregating the children from L1 speakers of the language and therefore underexposing them to the target language. A school that is language aware and whose teachers evaluate students in terms of their individual development will not lock their students into ability language groups where the richness of talk will be limited. International Schools that think in terms of mixed ability groups allow for a range of achievement level within each group and therefore permit ESL learners to have access to a richer English language environment.

### What criteria do teachers use for grading school work?

Many International Schools send home reports with letter grades or percentages. It is important for parents to know what these mean. It is also important for both the student and parent to know and understand how the grades are arrived at and calculated. Most International Schools grade ESL children on both effort and achievement. ESL children may come from national systems where every mistake is corrected. There are some International Schools that also use this form of overt correction. Many, however, make a conscious effort to focus on the meaning of what is being said and written rather than on the correctness of language per se.

Judy Jameson (1999) has identified a list of issues that teachers face when grading ESL children. These can be summarised as follows:

- the ESL student's limited English affects her ability to communicate her content knowledge;
- the ESL student works hard but the student's achievement falls short in comparison to others in the class because of her limited proficiency in English;
- the teacher's worry that recognising the student's effort and progress will be setting two standards of achievement in the class – ESL and non ESL;
- the teacher and the ESL student may have different expectations and interpretations of the grade.

Judy Jameson (1999) goes on to suggest how teachers can develop a grading and assessment plan that addresses these issues:

(1) Teachers can focus on the meaning instead of language errors such as grammar and syntax mistakes. Teachers can ask themselves: did the student understand the question? How well did the student develop her thoughts?

(2) Teachers can grade using a combination of process (how) and product (what is done) for all students. Thomas Guskey illustrates this:

> Imagine two students in a gym class. One is a brilliant athlete; the other has poor movement skills but always tries her hardest and is always a good sport. If we use only end product criteria to judge such as how high the student can jump, how fast the student can run we are not recognizing the second student for the things she does well and which are equally worthwhile and relevant criteria for the class.
>
> (Quoted in Jameson, 1999)

(3) Teachers can explain to students what and how they grade. Show students examples of good work. Use scoring rubrics that explain clearly to students the criteria used for grading. Teachers can also involve students in developing criteria for evaluating assessments and also teach students to evaluate their own work.

(4) Teachers can ensure that grades reflect a variety of performances e.g. participation projects, portfolios and oral explanations.

(5) Teachers can adapt test content and the way tests are carried out. They can allow ESL children more time, read the test to them, perhaps using other words if they don't understand the written language of the test. They can also teach test-taking skills and strategies. (Grading on a curve is often unfair to ESL students as it compares them to other children. Criterion-referenced tests are fairer as they test the students in terms of their mastery of a subject, not necessarily of the language used.)

(6) Teachers can teach students to evaluate their own work. It is important to talk to students about grading especially if the teacher thinks the students' expectations were different from the grade they received.

(7) Teachers can grade beginning ESL students as satisfactory, unsatisfactory or at/above/below expectations.

(8) Teachers can put a note on the report card to identify the student as an ESL learner and write comments to clarify how the student was graded.

Two more points that may be added to Jameson's list are:

(9) Teachers can accept brainstorming, mind mapping and any evidence of planning in the child's first language.

(10) Teachers can talk children through their report cards making sure that they understand the comments made. This can be done using the child's mother-tongue if necessary.

Teachers need to use a variety of assessments and when teachers use traditional tests such as multiple choice, they must check that the language and cultural bias has been minimised.

Evidence for second language acquisition is . . .

- what students say;
- what they write;
- what they read;
- what they can do.

Teachers who keep a 'can do list' for their ESL students will avoid focusing on what ESL students can't do.

It used to be considered that knowing a language or having proficiency in a language was a matter of knowing the grammatical rules and vocabulary that could be tested by measuring the learner's grammatical and lexical knowledge. However knowledge of a language and proficiency in its use are not the same. You can have knowledge of a language and be able to recall and apply grammatical rules and yet not be proficient in the sense of being able to use the language for communication. Today there is a trend to look at:

- what learners can do with language;
- the tasks they carry out;
- how they carry them out.

Teachers should focus on total language behaviour more than on its component parts and they need to assess the behaviour in authentic situations.

### How does the school assess ESL children in mainstream classes?

There are International Schools that place ESL children in mainstream classes and make very few accommodations for the ESL learner. They may be given the same tests as the other students and invariably get lower grades. Some schools do not grade ESL children for the first year of mainstreaming. Others have ESL children take tests to give them practice in test-taking but do not record the grades. In International Schools where administrators and teachers are more informed on language issues mainstream teachers use performance assessment tasks. These kinds of tasks ask students to create products, conduct experiments, debate, write, do projects, hold exhibitions, etc. Students are asked to do something with their knowledge not just simply regurgitate it. This kind of testing sends a message to the students that the teacher values in-depth understanding, the ability to apply knowledge to new situations and high-quality work. Children are also more motivated to do this kind of assessment rather than to take a traditional test.

Here are some practical assessment tools used in classes in International Schools that successfully integrate the ESL child into the mainstream

*Portfolios*: A portfolio is a collection of a student's work that reflects growth and achievement of curriculum objectives over a period of time. The portfolio can be kept in a folder, bound like a book or even kept in a box. The teacher usually chooses the purpose, sets the timetable for a completion and determines who will evaluate the portfolio. The student usually selects the items to be included and explains why each is included. Some reasons the student might choose are:

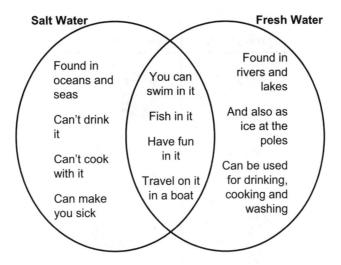

**Figure 20** A Venn diagram

- this is my best procedural writing (the writing up of an experiment etc.);
- this essay shows that I know how to write a factual recount (the writing up of a historical event);
- this one shows that I learnt how to show both sides of an argument (the writing of a discussion essay).

The student keeps the table of contents of the portfolio up to date and sets personal goals for learning. This type of assessment reveals very clearly how a student's academic performance grows over time and also teaches the student how to self-evaluate and reflect on her learning.

*Learning logs and journals*: Keeping a journal involves students writing a summary of what they have learnt in class in their own words. The summaries in the journal create a personal record of learning over time. Students can also use the journals to have a dialogue with their teachers using the themes from class. Teachers can use these contributions to assess the student's comprehension of content.

*Graphic organisation and Venn diagrams*: Students can compare two concepts, ideas, books in any content area using a Venn diagram, (two overlapping circles) or a T-chart (a page with a large T drawn on it). Figures 20 and 21 provide examples.

This kind of assessment focuses student attention on ideas and reduces concerns with language. There is no need for the student to write in complete sentences to show what she knows. Graphic organisers can be used to help ESL students participate and understand better even when their knowledge of the language is quite limited. It also provides them with the opportunity to use higher order thinking skills.

*Projects*: Students can research a topic and show, through oral presentations, written

**Figure 21**  A T-Chart

products, retellings, drawings and demonstrations, what they know and have learnt. Projects require the use of skills and knowledge similar to the way they are used in real-life situations. The work can involve parents and final products can be exhibited in the classroom. The work can be evaluated by the teacher, the student herself and by her peers.

*Self Assessment*: Students are active participants in deciding what and how to learn. Students can develop rubrics with teachers, for example they decide together how something will be graded, what criteria will be used and what points will be awarded. This helps students to know and understand what they should be able to do step-by-step through a unit and what is required at the end. The student also feels she has a say in her own learning.

Here are some examples of authentic assessment. Parents who want to know if their child is being assessed appropriately should look for key words in the school's assessment documents such as:

- teacher observation;
- anecdotal records;
- self-assessment;
- peer assessment;
- performance assessment;
- portfolio assessment.

A key element in authentic evaluation of ESL children is the use of multiple assessment techniques that provide the children with varied opportunities to show their learning and their accomplishments in a variety of ways.

## Questions to ask about the curriculum

*What curriculum is used in your school?*

Ask the school to explain the origin of its curriculum to you. Who developed the curriculum: the school or an outside authority? In effective schools teachers and administrators work as a team to implement and review the curriculum.

Some International Schools use national curricula such as the British National Curriculum, others might use state-based curriculum such as the Florida Sunshine State Standards. There are schools that develop their own curriculum and others that follow international curricula such as the IB. Some International Schools use the IB curriculum the whole way through, the IB PYP, MYP and the IBD. Other International Schools choose only to use this programme at the diploma level, that is, only in the last two years of high school.

It is important to establish that there is evidence in a school's curriculum that ESL children's needs are taken seriously. Ask schools to explain why and how their curriculum is relevant for a child whose first language is not English.

*My job causes me to travel a lot. Will my child's learning at your school be relevant to what she will study in successive International Schools?*

This concern about curricular continuity is a major one. Many teachers, administrators and students stay in International Schools for relatively short periods of time. This poses a difficult task for those schools trying to create and develop their own curriculum and programmes. If you are part of the international mobile workforce then you should place your child in an International School that follows the IB curriculum or, if your child is between the ages of 3 and 12, you can also consider putting her in an IPC school. A growing number of schools are taking on these international programmes making it possible for international children to have curricular continuity while they travel around the globe.

*What is the role of language in the curriculum?*

It is important that parents become familiar with the school's language policy to establish what is the actual use of language throughout the curriculum. Ask to read the language policy – some International Schools may not have one, others may have a brief paragraph. There are International Schools, however, that have given this a great deal of thought and have involved both parents and teachers in the articulation of the policy. It is important to find out, for example, whether teachers support the development of their students' mother-tongues in mainstream classes. Is the use of bilingual dictionaries and other bilingual texts encouraged? Some International Schools have language policies that explicitly state that mother-tongue languages are used for enrichment of learning in the mainstream classrooms. On the other hand, there are International Schools that choose to avoid the issue of mother-tongue usage in school and have no mention of mother-tongue in their language policies. Choose a school with a well thought out, coherent language policy that supports the development of all of your child's languages, especially her first one.

*Are children who are still learning English required to study the host country or foreign languages?*

There are International Schools that timetable ESL classes at the time when other students are studying host country or foreign language classes. Other schools insist that all children learn the host country language (sometimes this is imposed by local law). Some International Schools use the time allotted for foreign language learning for mother-tongue language instruction. Do not worry if your child is required to study another foreign language as well as English. The human brain has no problem absorbing multiple languages provided they are taught appropriately. In some countries students become fluent in three or more languages. Placing a beginner ESL child in a beginner foreign language class can be a highly rewarding experience for the child. It may be the only time of the day that she has the same language status as her peers. The child is a beginner amongst other beginners. If the child is placed in a host country language class this can help her adjust more quickly to the culture of the host country – particularly if meaningful language is taught, enabling the child to integrate, watch and understand television and play with her neighbours.

*What exams and tests are taken at the school?*

Some International Schools allow host country nationals to study for and take state exams during school time. Other schools propose that this happens out of school. There are International Schools that follow the British National Curriculum and may or may not used standardised tests on children aged 7, 11 and 14 to see how their children compare to those in Britain. Some 'British-style' International Schools prepare children for IGCSE (the International General Certificate of Secondary Education) at the age of 16 and A-level (Advanced level) subjects at 18. Students usually choose around three subjects to take at Advanced level. There are 'American-style' International Schools that prepare their students to take College Board PSAT (Preliminary Scholastic Aptitude Tests) in grades 10 and 11. These are considered practice tests for the SAT (Scholastic Aptitude Test), which is taken in the final year of high school. This test aims to measure critical thinking skills, mathematical reasoning and writing skills for students who will need to do college level work. American-style International Schools may also offer Advanced Placement (AP) exams. These are generally thought of as being more demanding than regular high school classes and are comparable to first-year college courses in America.

There are International Schools that offer the possibility of doing these tests and the IBD. Some schools offer the full IBD or the opportunity to obtain an IB certificate in individual subject areas. In certain International Schools students are screened and selected for the IBD programme. In other schools all children are registered in the programme.

The IBO works with many schools around the world. In order to obtain the IBD, students study six academic subjects concurrently. At least three of these (and no more than four) are taken as higher level subjects and the others at standard level.

Some International Schools offer the IBO's MYP to students aged 11 to 16 years as a preparation for the IBD. Students' accomplishments are measured through ongoing assessment and recorded in a portfolio of achievement. There are International Schools that subscribe to all of the IB programmes and others that subscribe to one or two of the three programmes.

Whilst it is important to ask about examination results, it is equally valid to remember that exam results are not the only criteria to be used when choosing an International School.

Ask the school if you can look at course content. Try and ascertain that the content provides an international perspective. At an elementary level, check to see if the curriculum is made up of units of work based around themes of intrinsic interest to children. Thematic units of work lend themselves to better integration of the ESL child than do classes that use a rigid, textbook orientation. Themes allow ESL learners to be successful in their own way. A beginner ESL child may produce a word or draw a picture connected to the theme whilst others in the class write sentences or paragraphs. Themes allow the ESL learners to fit in, exposing them to the same learning as their peers even when they still have a low level of proficiency in English.

It is also important to consider how classes are set up. Are classes laid out in the traditional format of desks in a row one behind the other, all facing the teacher's desk? Or are desks grouped in clusters suggesting that the students regularly work using collaborative learning strategies. A natural learning environment is interactive. ESL learners are often shy and insecure in their use of English. To flourish they need an environment that encourages risk-taking and lots of talking. They may not be successful in a textbook or exam-driven classroom.

## Questions to ask about fees

*Do the school tuition fees include the teaching of English as a second language?*

There are schools that charge extra fees for ESL lessons but there are a large number of schools that do not. Refuse a school that asks for more money so your child can receive ESL instruction and look for a school that considers ESL as an integral part of the curriculum.

*Does the school charge more for mother-tongue lessons?*

Most International Schools that provide mother-tongue instruction help parents only with the logistics. The fees for mother-tongue instruction are considered extra and paid for by the parents privately.

*My child has learning difficulties and will need the help of a resource teacher. Will I have to pay more for this?*

Many International Schools now have learning resource specialists on the staff and usually do not charge parents more for such classes. However, often screening and testing is required to ascertain how to help the child and this may be done by experts outside the school and often at considerable extra expense to parents.

## Conclusion

ESL parents should choose an International School where they are sure their children will be included rather that excluded. Effective International Schools make inclusion a priority. To close this chapter, Figure 22 contains a checklist of features parents should be looking for.

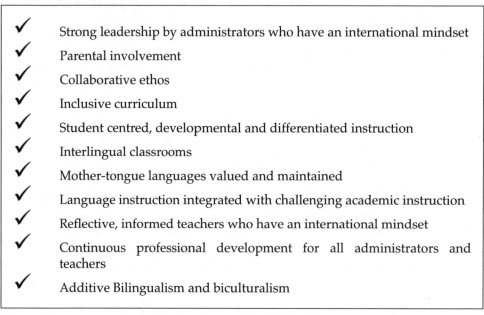

✓ Strong leadership by administrators who have an international mindset

✓ Parental involvement

✓ Collaborative ethos

✓ Inclusive curriculum

✓ Student centred, developmental and differentiated instruction

✓ Interlingual classrooms

✓ Mother-tongue languages valued and maintained

✓ Language instruction integrated with challenging academic instruction

✓ Reflective, informed teachers who have an international mindset

✓ Continuous professional development for all administrators and teachers

✓ Additive Bilingualism and biculturalism

**Figure 22**   Features of an effective International School

# Appendix 1: An Internationalism Audit

The following is the Internationalism Audit proposed by Michael Allan (2002, 2003) and mentioned in Chapter 1.

| 1. Peer Support | | | |
|---|---|---|---|
| Yes | Not yet | N/a | |
| | | | There is an organised peer tutoring and 'buddy' system which includes training and supervision. |
| | | | There is a peer mediation programme in the school. |
| | | | Care is taken to place students in classes and groups together with others of their own culture. |
| | | | Positive discrimination is practised in the appointment of positions of responsibility, school council, class representative etc. |
| | | | There are organised, vertically grouped study groups in the school for children of the same culture. |
| | | | Social and extra-curricular activities are arranged so as to give students the opportunity for inter-cultural learning. |
| | | | . . . |
| **2. Teacher Support** | | | |
| | | | Counsellors, heads of year, home room teachers etc. have the knowledge and skills required for effective cross-cultural counselling. |
| | | | Teachers take into account cultural differences in expectations, learning and teaching styles and assessment in their classes. |
| | | | Teachers use the students' own language wherever possible. |
| | | | Teachers make sure their instructions are understood by all students, including the use of written instructions when necessary. |
| | | | Expectations regarding student attendance and behaviour, homework, parental involvement etc. are realistic, negotiated and explicit. |
| | | | There is a procedure for conflict mediation when students experience racial or cultural discrimination or harassment in the school or beyond. |
| | | | Computers have different language keyboards and different language modules are installed. |
| | | | . . . |

| 3. Own Language Teaching | | | |
|---|---|---|---|
| Yes | Not yet | N/a | |
| | | | There is the opportunity for all students to study their mother-tongue within the curriculum, using distance learning via internet where on-site teaching is not available. |
| | | | The school library contains books in all the school languages and translating dictionaries for each language. |
| | | | Textbooks in students' mother-tongues are available. |
| | | | Students are encouraged to use their own language in writing for school publications and producing display material. |
| | | | Use is made of internet resources in students' native languages. |
| | | | Care is taken to ensure that mother-tongue teachers are welcomed as full members of the faculty. |
| | | | Parents and students are fully informed of the existence and benefits of the mother-tongue programme. |
| | | | . . . |
| **4. Effective ESL/EAL Programme** | | | |
| | | | Students are encouraged to participate in mainstream activities while learning Basic Interpersonal Communication Skills (BICS). |
| | | | EAL teachers team teach with class or subject teachers and assist in the preparation of lesson materials. |
| | | | EAL support in Cognitive and Academic Language Proficiency (CALP) continues throughout the students' school career. |
| | | | Mainstream teachers undergo training in EAL. |
| | | | Students are allowed to use translating dictionaries in lessons, and to work initially in their own language when appropriate. |
| | | | EAL students are grouped with more proficient English speakers from their own language background in cooperative learning activities. |
| | | | EAL student profiles are made available to mainstream teachers to assist in modifying teaching materials. |
| | | | . . . |
| **5. Cultural Affirmation** | | | |
| **5.1 Physical environment** | | | |
| | | | Signs, notices and displays in the school building are multilingual, and reflect a variety of cultural perspectives and positive images of different cultural groups. |
| | | | Guidelines for the selection and evaluation of resources include criteria related to cultural diversity. |

| Yes | Not yet | N/a | |
|---|---|---|---|
| | | | Classrooms contain visual and written material that represents various languages and cultures. |
| | | | School information, magazines, newsletters include content in different languages. |
| | | | Resource materials in different languages are available in the library |
| | | | Students and parents are involved in selecting resource material. |
| | | | . . . |

**5.2 Social environment**

| | | | |
|---|---|---|---|
| | | | Students' cultural and religious traditions and practices are maintained and respected as part of school life. |
| | | | Students' mothe- tongues are used in school announcements, parents' meetings and interviews. |
| | | | All students have opportunities to meet role models and mentors of different cultural backgrounds. |
| | | | All teachers in the school know something about the naming practices and forms of address that are usual in the various school communities. |
| | | | Students are encouraged to make natural language choices in social interaction around the school. |
| | | | . . . |

**6. Induction Procedures**

**6.1 Pre-arrival**

| | | | |
|---|---|---|---|
| | | | New students are contacted by email or letter by 'buddies' in the school. |
| | | | Families receive details of the academic programme, explaining differences from other academic models. |
| | | | Information sent to families includes information about the students and the school, such as photos, maps, school newspaper, yearbook etc. |
| | | | Families receive information on school procedure, times, rules, sports, extra-curricular activities local transport arrangements etc. |
| | | | Families receive information about the local culture and official government or ministry of education requirements. |
| | | | All of the above is available on the school website. |
| | | | . . . |

| 6.2 *Reception and orientation* | | | |
|---|---|---|---|
| Yes | Not yet | N/a | |
| | | | There is a planned programme of reception and orientation for students and parents, which includes orientation on classroom organisation and discourses, teaching and learning styles, assessment and homework, and general school procedure. |
| | | | Orientation materials are available in various languages. Interpreters and translators are available. |
| | | | Multilingual signs and notices welcome newcomers and provide directions. |
| | | | Parents are introduced to other families from their own culture and receive information about parent organisations and activities.. |
| | | | Parents receive information about and school staff communicate support for maintenance of mother-tongue learning. |
| | | | Parents receive information about ESL programme for adults. |
| | | | New students receive a 'starter kit' when they enter the school. |
| | | | . . . |
| 6.3. *Initial assessment and placement* | | | |
| | | | The school has a planned procedure for the assessment of each new student, using where necessary criteria relevant to students who are learning English, using tasks and materials that are likely to be familiar or in the student's mother-tongue. |
| | | | There is a procedure to assess the student's level of proficiency in the mother-tongue. |
| | | | Assessment of proficiency in English includes listening, speaking, reading and writing. |
| | | | Students with special needs are assessed in consultation with a bilingual educator who is familiar with the student's educational background. |
| | | | . . . |
| 7. *Social and Extra-curricular Activities* | | | |
| | | | Extra-curricular activities allow students to mix vertically and across friendship groups outside the normal school environment. |
| | | | There is cultural diversity in the nature of extra-curricular activities. |
| | | | Students and parents are consulted about their preferences and interests in extra-curricular activities. |
| | | | Students from mainstream cultures are encouraged to take part in extra-curricular activities from other cultures |

| Yes | Not yet | N/a | |
|-----|---------|-----|---|
| | | | Extra-curricular activities including students and using resources and members of the host culture are promoted. |
| | | | . . . |

**8. Intercultural Learning in the Curriculum**

| | | | |
|-----|---------|-----|---|
| | | | There is a post of responsibility in the school to coordinate ICL through the curriculum. |
| | | | ICL is included in the curriculum. |
| | | | Community service activities involve all students in the local community. |
| | | | Intercultural awareness is enhanced through activities, games and simulations in home rooms/tutorials. |
| | | | Students are encouraged to use and share their own cultures as contexts for learning. |
| | | | Parents, teachers and other members of different cultures are invited to give workshops and presentations to students about their own culture. |
| | | | The host culture is studied and there are opportunities for students to participate in host culture activities and for host culture students to participate in school activities. |
| | | | . . . |

**9. In-service Intercultural Teacher Training**

| | | | |
|-----|---------|-----|---|
| | | | All teachers are required to follow a cross-cultural training course on or prior to taking up their appointment. |
| | | | Teachers and support staff follow in-service training courses in intercultural awareness/attend intercultural awareness workshops at conferences. |
| | | | Teachers following international education post-graduate courses give in-service training workshops. |
| | | | Mother-tongue teachers give seminars on education in their home countries. |
| | | | Teachers are encouraged to take part in exchange programmes with teachers in other countries/the host country. |
| | | | Teachers are encouraged to learn the language of the host country. |
| | | | . . . |

**10. ...**

| | | | |
|-----|---------|-----|---|
| | | | |

# Glossary

The glossary gives further information about some terms used in this book. It also includes terms not used in this but regularly found in other books for parents and teachers on bilingualism.

**Accent:** People's pronunciation which may reveal, for example, which region, country or social class they come from.

**Acculturation:** The process by which an individual or a group adapt to a new culture.

**Acquisition Planning:** Part of formal language planning where interventions are made to encourage families to pass on their minority language, and schools to produce more minority language speakers.

**Active Vocabulary:** This refers to the actual number of words that people use as opposed to a passive vocabulary which is words they understand. Native language speakers often have an active vocabulary of between 30,000 and 50,000 words. Their passive vocabulary may extend up to 100,000 words or more. In foreign language learning, reasonable proficiency is said to be achieved when someone attains an active vocabulary of between 3000 and 5000 words with a passive vocabulary of up to 10,000 words.

**Additive Bilingualism:** A situation where a second language is learnt by an individual or a group without detracting from the development of the first language. A situation where a second language adds to, rather than replaces the first language. This is the opposite of subtractive bilingualism.

**Affective Filter:** Associated with Krashen's Monitor Model of second language learning, the affective filter is a metaphor which describes a learner's attitudes that affect the relative success of second language acquisition. Negative feelings such as a lack of motivation, lack of self-confidence and learning anxiety are like a filter which hinders and obstructs language learning.

**Anomie:** A feeling of disorientation and rootlessness, for example in in-migrant groups. A feeling of uncertainty or dissatisfaction in relationships between an individual learning a language and the language group with which they are trying to integrate.

**Aphasia:** Damage to the brain which causes a loss of ability to use and understand language. This may be partial or total and affect spoken and/or written language.

**Artificial Language:** (1) A language invented as a means of international communication (e.g. Esperanto, Ido). (2) A system of communication created for a specific purpose (e.g. computer language).

**Assimilation:** The process by which a person or language group lose their own language and culture which are replaced by a different language and culture. A political policy that seeks to absorb in-migrants into the dominant language and culture of the new country to create cultural and social unity.

**Authentic Texts:** Texts taken from newspapers, magazines, tapes of natural speech from radio and television. They are not created by the teacher but already exist in the world outside the classroom.

**Autochthonous Languages:** A term particularly used in Europe to describe indigenous languages or languages resident for a considerable length of time in a territory or region.

**Auxiliary Language:** (1) A language used as a means of communication between different language groups. See also lingua franca, pidgin, language of wider communication. (2) An artificial language invented as a means of communication between different language groups.

**Back Translation:** A translation is translated back into the original to assess the accuracy of the first translation.

**Balanced Bilingualism:** Approximately equal competence in two languages.

**Basal Readers:** Reading texts that use simplified vocabulary and grammar, carefully graded and structured.

**BEA:** Bilingual Education Act (United States legislation: part of ESEA).

**BICS:** Basic Interpersonal Communicative Skills. Everyday, straightforward communication skills that are helped by contextual supports.

**Bicultural:** Identifying with the culture of two different language groups. To be bilingual is not necessarily the same as being bicultural.

**Big Books:** Used frequently in 'whole language classrooms'. They are teachers' books that are physically big so that students can read along with the teacher.

**Biliteracy:** Reading and writing in two languages.

**Black English:** The variety of English spoken by some black people in the United States, for example in cities such as New York and Chicago. Black English is regarded as a language variety in its own right with its own structure and system and not as a second class variety of English.

**Borrowing:** A word or a phrase from one language that has become established in use in another language. When borrowing is a single word, it is often called a loan word.

**CABE:** California Association of Bilingual Education.

**CALL:** Computer Assisted Language Learning.

**CALP:** Cognitive/Academic Language Proficiency. The level of language required to understand academically demanding subject matter in a classroom. Such language is often abstract, without contextual supports such as gestures and the viewing of objects.

**Caretaker Speech:** A simplified language used by parents to children to ensure understanding, also called Motherese. Caretaker Speech usually has short sentences, is grammatically simple, has few difficult words, much repetition and with clear pronunciation.

**Classroom Discourse:** A special type of language used in the classroom. Such language is governed by the different roles that students and teachers assume and the kind of activities that occur in classrooms. The kind of 'open' (many different answers possible) or 'closed' questions (only one or a few correct answers possible) that teachers ask is one particular area of interest in Classroom Discourse.

**Classroom Ethos:** The atmosphere and feelings in the classroom that promote or detract from effective classroom learning.

**Classroom Interaction:** The interaction and relationships between teachers and students, and between students themselves both in terms of oral, written and non-verbal communication.

**Cloze Procedure:** A technique for measuring students' reading comprehension. In a Cloze test, words are removed from a reading passage at specific intervals, and students have to fill in the blanks. The missing words are guessed from the context.

**Codemixing:** The mixing of two languages within a sentence or across sentences.

**Codeswitching:** Moving from one language to another, inside a sentence or across sentences.

**Codification:** A systematic description of a variety of a language (e.g. vocabulary, grammar). This may occur when a language is being standardized, or when an oral language is being written down for the first time.

**Cognition:** The acquisition, storage, retrieval and use of knowledge. Mental processes of perception, memory, thinking, reasoning and language.

**Cognitive/Academic Language Proficiency (CALP):** The level of second language proficiency needed by students to perform the more abstract and cognitively demanding tasks of a classroom. Little support is offered in many classrooms from the context. CALP is distinguished from Basic Interpersonal Communication Skills (BICS), that are relatively undemanding cognitively and rely on the context to aid understanding.

**Cognitive Style:** The way in which different learners efficiently and effectively learn. Different students have different preferences, patterns and styles of learning.

**Common Underlying Proficiency (CUP):** Two languages working integratively in the thinking system. Each language serves one underlying, central thinking system.

**Communal Lessons:** Lessons in which students of different first languages are mixed for common activities, such as working on projects, doing art or physical education. The European Hours in the European Schools are Communal Lessons.

**Communicative Approach:** A second language teaching approach that accents the acquisition of a language by use in everyday communicative situations.

**Communicative Competence:** Proficiency in the use of a language in everyday conversations. This term accents being understood rather than being 'correct' in using a language. Not only knowing the grammar and vocabulary of a language, but also knowing the social and culturally appropriate uses of a language.

**Community Language:** A language used by a particular community or in a particular area, often referring to language minority groups. The term has been used in Britain to refer to the language of Asian and European groups which are resident in particular areas.

**Community Language Learning:** A second language teaching methodology based on Rogerian counseling techniques and responding to the needs of the learner 'community'.

**Competence in Language:** A person's ability to create and understand language. This goes further than an understanding of vocabulary and grammar, requiring the listener to understand sentences not heard before. The term is often used in association with Chomsky's theory of transformational grammar, describing a person's internalized grammar of the language, which enables the person to create and interpret new sentences. Competence is often used to describe an idealized speaker/hearer with a complete knowledge of the whole language, and is distinguished from performance which is the actual use of the language by individuals.

**Compound Bilingualism:** One language is learnt at the same time as another, often in the same contexts. Therefore, the representation in the brain was thought to be fused and interdependent.

**Comprehensible Input:** Language delivered at a level understood by a learner, often containing a few new elements.

**Concept:** The idea or meaning associated with a word or symbol in a person's thinking system. All languages can express the same concepts, although different languages construct concepts in different ways (e.g. languages tend to distinguish colors on the color spectrum in different ways).

**Content-Based Instruction:** A term particularly used in United States education programs. Such a program teaches students the language skills they will need in mainstream classrooms. The focus is on the language skills needed for content areas such as mathematics, geography, social studies and science.

**Content Reading:** The reading of books to learn particular curriculum areas as separate from reading for enjoyment only.

**Context:** The setting in which communication occurs, and which places possibilities and constraints on what is said, and how it is said. The context can refer to the physical setting or to the language context in which a word or utterance occurs.

**Context-Embedded Language:** Communication occurring in a context that offers help to comprehension (e.g. visual clues, gestures, expressions, specific location). Language where there are plenty of shared understandings and where meaning is relatively obvious due to help from the physical or social nature of the conversation.

**Context-Reduced Language:** Language where there are few clues as to the meaning of the communication apart from the words themselves. The language is likely to be abstract.

**Contrastive Analysis:** The comparison of the linguistic systems of two languages.

**Co-ordinate Bilingualism:** Two languages learnt in different and separate environments. The two languages were therefore once thought to be independent (e.g. in representation in the brain).

**Core Language Class:** Teaching the language as a subject. Used mostly to describe foreign language instruction.

**Core Subject:** A subject that is of prime importance in the Curriculum. In England, the three core subjects are Mathematics, English and Science. These are said to form the Core Curriculum.

**Corpus Language Planning:** Language planning which centers on linguistic aspects of language, vocabulary and grammar; for example, to try and ensure a normative or standardized system of language within an area (see also Language Planning).

**Creole:** A pidgin language which has been adopted as the native language in a region. A creole tends to be more complex in grammar with a wider range of vocabulary than a pidgin language. There are, for example, English-based and French-based Creoles.

**Creolization:** The process by which a pidgin becomes a creole by the expansion of vocabulary and the development of a more complex linguistic structure.

**Criterion-Referenced Testing:** A form of educational assessment which compares students in terms of their mastery of a subject as opposed to a norm-referenced test where a student is compared with other students. A criterion-referenced test in language requires a clear specification of the structure of the language to be learnt.

**Critical Period Hypothesis:** A genetically determined period of child development when learning must take place, otherwise it will not be learned later. In language, this is a largely discredited theory that a child best learns a first or second language between birth and up to about 13 years of age.

**Cultural Pluralism:** The ownership of two or more sets of cultural beliefs, values and attitudes. Multicultural education is often designed to encourage cultural pluralism in children.

**Culture:** The set of meanings, beliefs, attitudes, customs, everyday behavior and social understandings of a particular group, community or society.

**Culture Shock:** Feelings of disorientation, anxiety or insecurity some people experience when entering a different culture. For example, when people move to a foreign country there may be a period of culture shock until they become more familiar with a new culture.

**CUP:** See Common Underlying Proficiency.

**DBE:** Developmental Bilingual Education: Also known as Two-Way Dual Language Programs and Two-Way Bilingual/Immersion Programs. Two languages are used for approximately equal time in the curriculum.

**Decoding:** In learning to read, decoding is the deciphering of the sounds and meanings of letters, combinations of letters, whole words and sentences of text. Sometimes decoding refers to being able to read a text without necessarily understanding the meaning of that text.

**Deficit Model:** The idea that some children have a deficiency in their language – in vocabulary, grammar or understanding, particularly in the classroom. The child has a perceived language 'deficit' that has to be compensated for by remedial schooling or compensatory education. The problem is seen to be located in the child rather than in the school system or society or in the ideology of the perceiver. The opposite is an enrichment model (see Enrichment Bilingual Education).

**Developmental Bilingual Education:** A US program that encourages bilingualism and biliteracy by including development of native language and literacy (e.g. Spanish). Such a program may last for five years and more.

**Dialect:** A language variety whose features identify the regional or social background of the user. The term is often used in relation to a standard variety of a language (e.g. a dialect of English).

**Diglossia:** Two languages or language varieties existing together in a society in a stable arrangement through different uses attached to each language.

**Discourse:** A term used to describe relatively large chunks of conversation or written text. Rather than highlighting vocabulary or grammar, discourse extends into understandings and meanings of conversation or written text.

**Discourse Analysis:** The study of spoken and written language particularly in terms of negotiated meanings between participants in speech, choice of linguistic forms, shared assumptions that underlie utterances, structures, strategies and symbolism in communicating, and the role relationships between participants.

**Disembedded Thinking:** Thinking that is not allied to a meaningful context but is treated as a separate, distinct task with little relevance in itself.

**Distance Learning:** Independent learning outside the classroom, by telephone, satellite, the world wide web and distance learning packages, for example.

**Divergent Thinking:** Thinking that is original, imaginative and creative. A preference for open-ended, multiple answers to questions.

**Domain:** Particular contexts where a language is used. For example, there is the family domain where a minority language may be used. In the work domain, the majority language may be used.

**Dominant Language:** The language which a person has greater proficiency in or uses more often.

**Double Immersion:** Schooling where subject content is taught through a second and third language (e.g. Hebrew and French for first language English speakers).

**Dual Language Program:** see Two-Way Programs.

**Dyslexia:** Problems in learning to read; word blindness where students may have difficulty in, for example, distinguishing different letter shapes and words.

**Early-Exit/Late-Exit Bilingual Education Programs:** Early-exit programs move children from bilingual classes in the first or second year of schooling. Late-exit programs provide bilingual classes for three or more years of elementary schooling. Both programs are found in Transitional Bilingual Education.

**EC:** European Community. A grouping of most European countries for mutual economic, social and cultural benefit.

**Eclectic Method:** Using a variety of methods in language teaching.

**EEC:** European Economic Community. A grouping of European countries, accenting economic cooperation. This term has largely been superseded by EU (European Union).

**EFL:** English as a Foreign Language.

**ELL:** English Language Learners. This is sometimes preferred to LEP (Limited English Proficiency) as it focuses on development rather than deficit.

**ELT:** English language teaching.

**Empowerment:** The means by which those of low status, low influence and power are given the means to increase their chances of prosperity, power and prestige. Literacy and biliteracy are major means of empowering such individuals and groups.

**English-Only:** An umbrella term for federal and state legislation and organizations that aim to make English the official language of the US. This includes two national organizations: US English and English First.

**English Plus:** A US movement promoting the belief that all US residents should have the opportunity to become proficient in a language other than English.

**Enrichment Bilingual Education:** A form of bilingual education that seeks to develop additive bilingualism, thus enriching a person's cultural, social and personal education. Two languages and cultures are developed through education.

**Equilingual:** Someone who is approximately equally competent in two languages.

**ERA:** The 1988 Education Reform Act (UK).

**ERASMUS:** A European program for students to take part of their higher education at one or more European universities or colleges as well as their 'home' University or College.

**ESEA:** Elementary and Secondary Education Act (United States).

**ESL:** English as a Second Language. An ESL program (e.g. in the US) usually involves little or no use of the first language, and occurs for part of the school timetable.

**ESOL:** English for Speakers of Other Languages.

**ESP:** English for Special Purposes. For example, English may be taught for its use in the Science and Technology curriculum, or English for business, specific vocational needs and professions.

**Ethnic Identity:** Those aspects of an individual's thinking, feelings, perceptions and behavior that are due to ethnic group membership, as well as a sense of belonging and pride in the ethnic group.

**Ethnic Mosaic:** In-migrants of different geographical origins co-existing in a country (e.g. Canada, United States) and retaining constituents of their ethnicity.

**Ethnocentrism:** Discriminatory beliefs and behaviours based on ethnic differences. Evaluating other ethnic groups by criteria specific to one's own group.

**Ethnographic Pedagogy:** Teaching practices and learning strategies that are derived from ethnography (see below) and conducted in the classroom. An ethnographic researcher becomes involved in a classroom, observing, participating and helping transform teaching practices. Ethnographic pedagogy includes learning to read by harnessing students' prior cultural knowledge and experience, and encouraging peer interaction.

**Ethnography:** Research that describes and analyzes groups (e.g. ethnic, cultural) and is qualitative rather than quantitative in approach (e.g. engages in fieldwork, interviews and observation). Such research is often intensive and detailed, hence small-scale.

**Ethnography of Communication:** The study of the place of language in different groups and communities. Language is particularly studied for its social and cultural purposes.

**Ethnolinguistic:** A set of cultural, ethnic and linguistic features shared by a cultural, ethnic, or sub-cultural social group.

**EU:** European Union. A recent term to describe the grouping of European countries for mutual benefit.

**FEP:** Fluent English Proficient.

**First Language:** This term is used in different, overlapping ways, and can mean (a) the first language learnt, (b) the stronger language, (c) the 'mother tongue' (d) the language most used.

**FLAP:** The Foreign Language Assistance Program authorized under Title VII of the Improving America's Schools Act of 1994, that awards grants to US states and local educational agencies to promote programs that improve foreign language learning.

**Flexible Learning:** The provision of materials for learners to be used independently with minimal guidance and direction from a teacher.

**Foreigner Talk:** The kind of speech used by native speakers when talking to foreigners who are not proficient in their language. Foreigner talk is often slower, with clear pronunciation, simplified vocabulary and grammar with some degree of repetition. This makes the speech easier for foreigners to understand.

**Foreign Language:** A language taught in school which is not normally used as a mean of instruction in schools or as a language of communication within the country, in the community or in bureaucracy.

**Funds of Knowledge:** Knowledge that exists in communities and individuals outside of school that is valuable to share. Such knowledge particularly derives from language and cultural minorities and is not transmitted in a majority language school curriculum.

**Gastarbeiter:** (German term) An in-migrant or guestworker.

**Gemeinschaft:** A society based on close community bonds, kinship, close family ties; an emphasis on tradition and heritage. Sometimes portrayed stereotypically as village life.

**Geolinguistics:** The study of language or dialects as spoken in different geographical areas and regions. Sometimes referred to as Areal Linguistics.

**Gesellschaft:** A society with less emphasis on tradition and more on rational goals; duty to organizations with many secondary relationships. Sometimes portrayed stereotypically as one type of urban existence.

**Graded Objectives:** Objectives in a language curriculum which describe levels of attainment at different stages. These provide short-term, immediate goals for learners who are required to gain mastery of these goals before moving on to higher objectives.

**Graded Reader:** A simplified book or set of children's books, carefully graded in terms of increasingly difficult vocabulary and complexity of grammar. Such books are written for first language learners, adult second language learners and students learning a second language. In order to control the linguistic features precisely, authenticity may be sacrificed.

**Grammar:** The structure of a language; the way in which elements are combined to make words and the way in which words and phrases are combined to produce sentences.

**Graphology:** The study of systems of writing and the way a language is written.

**Guest Workers:** People who are recruited to work in another society. Also known as Gastarbeiter.

**Hegemony:** Domination; the ascendance of one group over another. The dominant group expects compliance and subservience from the subordinate group.

**Heritage Language:** The language a person regards as their native, home, ancestral language. This covers indigenous languages (e.g. Welsh in Wales) and in-migrant languages (e.g. Spanish in the United States).

**Heterogeneous Grouping:** The use of mixed ability and / or mixed language groups or classes. The opposite is 'homogeneous grouping' or tracking (see below).

**Hispanics:** Spanish speakers in the United States. The term is, for example, officially used in the United States Census.

**Immersion Bilingual Education:** Schooling where some or most subject content is taught through a second language. Pupils in immersion are usually native speakers of a majority language, and the teaching is carefully structured to their needs.

**Incipient Bilingualism:** The early stages of bilingualism where one language is not strongly developed. Beginning to acquire a second language.

**Indigenous Language:** A language relatively native to an area, contrasted with an in-migrant language.

**Individualized Instruction:** A curriculum which is carefully structured to allow for the different needs and pace of learning of different students. Individualized instruction tries to give learners more control over what is learned, the style of learning and the rate of progress.

**In-migrants:** Encompasses immigrants, migrants, guest workers and refugees. The term in-migrant can be used to avoid the negative connotations of the term 'immigrant' and to avoid the imprecise and loaded distinctions between migrant workers, guest workers, short-stay, long-stay and relatively permanent in-migrants.

**Input:** A distinction is often made in second language learning between input and intake. Input is what the learner hears but which may not always be understood. In contrast, intake is that which is assimilated by the learner.

**Input Hypothesis:** Language in the second language classroom should contain elements that are slightly beyond the learner's present level of understanding. Using contextual clues to understand, the learner will gradually increase in language competence.

**Institutionalized Racism:** Processes, attitudes and behavior in an organization that are discriminatory through unthinking prejudice, ignorance, thoughtlessness and racist stereotyping which disadvantage minority ethnic individuals and groups.

**Instrumental Motivation:** Wanting to learn a language for utilitarian reasons (e.g. to get a better job).

**Integrated Approach:** The integration of listening, speaking, reading and writing in language teaching and language assessment.

**Integrative Motivation:** Wanting to learn a language to belong to a social group (e.g. make friends).

**Interactionism:** A position which argues that language cannot be understood without reference to the social context in which language occurs.

**Interference:** Interference (or transfer) in second language learning is said to occur when vocabulary or syntax patterns transfer from a learner's first language to the second language, causing errors in second language performance. The term interference has been decreasingly used because of its negative and derogatory connotations. See Language Transfer.

**Interlanguage:** An intermediate form of language used by second language learners in the process of learning a language. Interlanguage contains some transfers or borrowing from the first language, and is an approximate system with regard to grammar and communicating meaning.

**Interlocutors:** Those who are actively engaged in a conversation as opposed to those who are silent participants.

**International Language:** A high prestige, majority language used as a means of communication between different countries speaking different languages (e.g. English, French, Spanish).

**Interpreting:** The process of oral translation from one language to another. Consecutive interpreting occurs when an interpreter orally translates while a speaker pauses. Simultaneous translation occurs when the interpreter orally translates while the speaker continues to speak. For example, an interpreter sits in a sound-proof booth, receiving the speaker's words through headphones. The translation is relayed to listeners via a microphone linked to listeners' headphones.

**Intranational Language:** A high prestige language used as a medium of general communication between different language groups within a country (e.g. English in India).

**Involuntary Minorities:** Also known as 'caste-like minorities'. They differ from immigrants and 'voluntary minorities' in that they have not willingly migrated to the country.

**Koine:** The spoken language of a region that has become a standard language or lingua franca.

**L1/L2:** First Language/Second Language.

**Language Ability:** An 'umbrella' term and therefore used ambiguously. Language ability is a general, latent disposition, a determinant of eventual language success. Language ability is also used to describe the outcome of language learning, in a similar but less specific way than language skills, providing an indication of current language level. Language ability measures what a person can currently do, as different from what they may be able to do in the future.

**Language Achievement:** Normally seen as the outcome of formal language instruction. Proficiency in a language due to what has been taught or learnt in a language classroom.

**Language Acquisition:** The process of acquiring a first or second language. Some linguists distinguish between language acquisition and 'language learning' of a second language, using the former to describe the informal development of a person's second language, and the latter to describe the process of formal study of a second language. Other linguists maintain that no clear distinction can be made between informal acquisition and formal learning.

**Language Across the Curriculum:** A curriculum approach to language learning that accents language development across all subjects of the curriculum. Language should be developed in all content areas of the curriculum and not just as a subject in its own right. Similar approaches are taken in writing across the curriculum and reading across the curriculum.

**Language Approach:** A term usually used in a broad sense to describe the theories and philosophies about the nature of language and how languages are learned, (e.g. aural/oral approach, communicative approach). The term 'method' is used to describe how languages are taught in the classroom, (e.g. audiolingual method), and the term 'techniques' is used to describe the activities involved (e.g. role playing, drill).

**Language Aptitude:** A particular ability to learn a language as separate from intelligence, motivation.

**Language Arts:** Those parts of the curriculum which focus on the development of language: reading, writing, spelling as well as oral communication.

**Language Attitudes:** The beliefs and values expressed by people towards different languages in terms of favorability and unfavorability.

**Language Attrition:** The loss of a language within a person or a language group, gradually over time.

**Language Awareness:** A comprehensive term used to describe knowledge about and appreciation of the attributes of a language, the way a language works and is used in society.

**Language Change:** Change in a language over time. All living languages are in a process of gradual change (e.g. in pronunciation, grammar, vocabulary).

**Language Code:** A neutral term used instead of language or speech or dialect.

**Language Competence:** A broad and general term, used particularly to describe an inner, mental representation of language, something latent rather than overt. Such competence refers usually to an underlying system inferred from language performance.

**Language Contact:** Contact between speakers of different languages, particularly when they are in the same region or in adjoining communities.

**Language Death:** Language death is said to occur when a declining language loses its last remaining speakers through their death or their shift to using another language.

This language no longer exists as a medium of communication in any language domains.

**Language Demographics:** The distribution of the use of a language in a defined geographical area. Also called Geolinguistics.

**Language Dominance:** One language being the stronger or preferred language of an individual, or the more prestigious language within a particular region.

**Language Family:** A group of languages historically derived from a common ancestor.

**Language Isolate:** A language isolate is a language that has no apparent relationship to any other known language.

**Language Laboratory:** A room with individual booths fitted with cassette recorders. Students listen to recorded tapes and practice speaking exercises which can be monitored by teachers. Recently, the room may have individual multimedia computer equipment for language learning.

**Language Learning:** The process by which a first or second language is internalized. Some authors restrict the use of the term to formal learning (e.g. in the classroom). Others include informal learning (e.g. acquisition in the home). See also Language Acquisition.

**Language Loss:** The process of losing the ability or use of a language within an individual or within a group. Language loss is particularly studied amongst in-migrants to a country where their mother tongue has little or no status, little economic value or use in education, and where language loss subsequently occurs.

**Language Loyalty:** The purposeful maintenance and retention of a language, when that language is viewed as being under threat. This is often a concern of language minorities in a region where another language is the dominant language.

**Language Maintenance:** The continued use of a language, particularly amongst language minorities (for example through bilingual education). The term is often used with reference to policies that protect and promote minority languages.

**Language Minority:** A language community (or person) whose first language is different from the dominant language of the country. A group who speaks a language of low prestige, or low in power, or with low numbers in a society.

**Language of Wider Communication:** A language used for communication within a region or country by different language groups.

**Language Performance:** A person's production of language particularly within a classroom or test situation. The outward evidence of language competence, but which is not necessarily an accurate measure of language competence.

**Language Planning:** The development of a deliberate policy to engineer the use of language. Language planning often involves Corpus Planning (the selection, codification and expansion of norms of language), Status Planning (the choice of language varieties for different functions and purposes) and Acquisition Planning (acquiring the language in the family and/or at school).

**Language Proficiency:** An 'umbrella' term, sometimes used synonymously with language competence; at other times as a specific, measurable outcome from language testing. Language proficiency is viewed as the product of a variety of mechanisms: formal learning, informal uncontrived language acquisition (e.g. on the street) and of individual characteristics such as 'intelligence'.

**Language Revitalization:** The process of restoring language vitality by promoting the use of a language and its range of functions within the community.

**Language Shift:** A change from the use of one language to another language within an individual or a language community. This often involves a shift from the minority language to the dominant language of the country. Usually the term means 'downward' shift (i.e. loss of a language).

**Language Skills:** Language skills are usually said to comprise: listening, speaking, reading and writing. Each of these can be divided into sub-skills. Language skills refer to specific, observable and clearly definable components such as writing.

**Language Transfer:** The effect of one language on the learning of another. There may be negative transfer, sometimes called interference, and much more often positive transfer, particularly in understandings and meanings of concepts.

**Language Variety:** A regionally or socially distinctive variety of language. A term used instead of 'dialect' because of the negative connotations of that term, and because 'dialect' is often used to indicate a hierarchical relationship with a standard form of a language.

**Language Vitality:** The extent to which a language minority vigorously maintains and extends its everyday use and range of functions. Language vitality is said to be enhanced by factors such as language status, institutional support, economic value and the size and distribution of its speakers.

**Latinos:** Spanish speakers of Latin American extraction. This Spanish term is now used in English, especially by US Spanish speakers themselves. Often preferred by such speakers to 'Hispanics'.

**Learning Journal:** Students record in a note book or log book their personal experiences in and out of school, and often record their responses and reactions to their reading and other curriculum activity. Such journals may be shared with the teacher who responds with a non-judgmental written reply. Journals aim to encourage students through personalization, increased motivation and enjoyable dialogue.

**LEP:** Limited English Proficient (US term). Used to refer to students in the United States who are not native speakers of English and who have yet to reach 'desired' levels of competence in understanding, speaking, reading or writing English. Such students are deemed to have insufficient English to cope in English-only classrooms.

**Lexical Competence:** Competence in vocabulary.

**Lexis/Lexicon:** The vocabulary or word stock of a language, their sounds, spelling and meaning.

**LINGUA:** A European program to increase majority language learning across Europe. The program funds scholarships, student exchanges and teaching materials to improve language learning and teaching in the European (EU) countries.

**Lingua Franca:** A language used for communication between different language groups. A lingua franca may be a local, regional, national or international language.

It may be the first language of one language group. Lingua francas are especially common in multilingual regions.

**Linguicism:** The use of ideologies, structures and practices to legitimize and reproduce unequal divisions of power and resources between language groups.

**Linguistic Purism:** A deliberate attempt to rid a language of perceived undesirable elements (e.g. dialect forms, slang, foreign loan words).

**Literacy:** The ability to read and write in a language.

**LM:** Language Minority.

**LMS:** Language Minority Students.

**Loan Word:** An item of vocabulary borrowed by one language from another. A loan blend occurs when the meaning is borrowed but only part of the form is borrowed; loan shift when the form is nativized; and loan translation when the components of a word are translated (e.g. 'skyscraper' into *'gratte ciel'* in French).

**Machine Translation:** Translation from one language to another by computer.

**Mainstreaming:** Putting a student who has previously been in a special educational program into ordinary classes. Language mainstreaming occurs when children are no longer given special support (e.g. English as a Second Language classes) and take their subjects through the majority language.

**Maintenance Bilingual Education:** A program that uses both languages of students to teach curriculum content.

**Majority Language:** A high status language usually (but not always) spoken by a majority of the population of a country. 'Majority' refers to status and power rather than the numerical size of a language group.

**Marked Language:** A minority language spoken by a minority of the population in a country (as distinct from a majority language), and therefore often lowly valued in society.

**Meaningful Learning:** Learning which becomes accommodated within a person's conceptual system. This has been distinguished from rote learning which is not necessarily integrated into existing conceptual understandings and may exist for a short, temporary period of time.

**Medium of Education:** The language used to teach content. Also medium of instruction.

**Medium of Instruction:** The language used to transmit instructional material.

**Melting Pot:** Used mainly in the US to describe how a variety of in-migrant ethnic groups have blended together to create modern US society.

**Message:** The meaning of a communication which may be conveyed in verbal form but also by non-verbal communication such as eye contact, gestures and posture. A distinction is often made between the form of message and message content. The form refers to how communication occurs and the content as to the meaning conveyed.

**Metacognition:** Becoming aware of one's own mental processes.

**Metalinguistic:** Using language to describe language. Thinking about one's language.

**Metalinguistic Knowledge:** An understanding of the form and structure of language arrived at through reflection and analyzing one's own communication.

**Minority Language:** A language of low prestige and low in power. Also usedby some to mean a language spoken by a minority of the population in a country.

**Miscue Analysis:** Analysis of errors and incorrect responses readers make in reading.

**Monitor Hypothesis:** A theory of second language developed by Krashen. According to this theory, language can only be acquired in a natural, unconscious manner. The consciously learned rules of language have the function of monitoring or editing communication. This involves monitoring one's own speech or writing, to ensure accuracy of form and meaning, making corrections where necessary.

**Monogenesis:** A theory that all the languages in the world derive historically from a single ancestor.

**Monoglot:** See monolingual.

**Monolingual:** A person who knows and/or uses one language.

**Morphology:** The internal structure of words (a morpheme is the smallest unit of meaning).

**Mother Tongue:** The term is used ambiguously. It variously means (a) the language learnt from the mother, (b) the first language learnt, irrespective of 'from whom', (c) the stronger language at any time of life, (d) the 'mother tongue' of the area or country (e.g. Irish in Ireland), (e) the language most used by a person, (f) the language to which a person has the more positive attitude and affection.

**Motherese:** A simplified language used by parents to children to ensure understanding. See Caretaker Speech.

**Multilingual:** A person who knows and/or uses three languages or more.

**NABE:** The National Association for Bilingual Education (NABE) is a US professional association of teachers, administrators, parents, policy makers and others concerned with securing educational equity for language minority students.

**National Language:** On the surface, this refers to a prestigious, authorized language of the nation, but the term has varying and debated meanings. Sometimes it is used interchangeably with 'official language'. However, in multilingual countries, an official language (or languages) may co-exist with one or more national languages. Such national languages are not so widely used in public and official use throughout the country, but carry symbolic status and prestige. Also, a national language may be formally recognized as such, or may be informally attributed as a national language.

**Native Language:** The language which a person acquires first in life, or identifies with as a member of an ethnic group.

**NCBE:** The National Clearinghouse for Bilingual Education is funded by the US Department of Education, Office of Bilingual Education and Minority Languages Affairs (OBEMLA) to collect, analyze, and disseminate information related to the education of linguistically and culturally diverse students.

**Negotiation:** Negotiation occurs in a conversation so that successful and smooth communication occurs. The use of feedback, corrections, exemplification, repetition, elaboration and simplification may aid negotiation.

**NEP:** Non-English Proficient.

**Network:** A group of people within a community who are regularly in communication with each other and whose manner of communication is relatively stable and enduring. Analysis of a language network examines different status relationships within the network.

**Non-Native Variety:** A language variety not indigenous to a region, but imported by in-migrants.

**Non-Verbal Communication:** Communication without words; for example, via gestures, eye contact, position and posture when talking, body movements and contact, tone of voice.

**OBEMLA:** The Office of Bilingual Education and Minority Languages Affairs in the US Department of Education, established in 1974 by Congress to provide equal educational opportunities for Limited English Proficient students.

**OCR:** Office of Civil Rights (United States).

**Official Language:** The language used in a region or country for public, formal and official purposes (e.g. government, administration, education, media).

**Orthography:** Correct spelling.

**Paired Reading:** Where parents share reading at home with their children, often with direction from the school, and sometimes using a reading scheme.

**Parallel Teaching:** Where bilingual children are taught by two teachers working together as a team, each using a different language. For example, a second language teacher and the class teacher planning together but teaching independently.

**Passive Bilingualism:** Being able to understand (and sometimes read) in a second language without speaking or writing in that second language.

**Personality Principle:** The right to use a language based on the history and character of the language, rather than a right to use that language based on territorial rights. See Territorial Principle.

**Phonetics:** The study of speech sounds.

**Phonics:** A method of teaching reading based on recognizing the sounds of letters and combinations of letters.

**Phonology:** The sound system of a language.

**Pidgin:** A language that develops as a means of communication when different language groups are in regular contact with one another. A pidgin usually has a small vocabulary and a simplified grammatical structure. Pidgins do not usually have native speakers although there are expanded pidgins, (for example, in Papua New Guinea) where a pidgin is the primary language of the community. If a pidgin language expands to become the native language of a group of speakers, with a larger vocabulary and a more complex structure, it is often called a creole.

**Pidginization:** (1) The evolution of a pidgin language. (2) In second and foreign language learning, the development of a simplified form of the target language (also called interlanguage). This intermediate stage is usually temporary, but according to the pidginization hypothesis, it may become permanent when learners remain socially apart from native speakers, or when the target language is infrequently used.

**Plurilingual:** Someone competent in two or more languages.

**Polyglot:** Someone competent in two or more languages.

**Pragmatics:** The study of the use of language in communication, with a particular emphasis on the contexts in which language is used.

**Preferred Language:** A self-assessment of the more proficient or favored language of an individual.

**Primary Bilingualism:** Where two languages have been learnt 'naturally' (not via school teaching, for example).

**Primary Language:** The language in which bilingual/multilingual speakers are most fluent, or which they prefer to use. This is not necessarily the language learnt first in life.

**Process Approach in Language Teaching:** This is particularly used in teaching children to write where planning, drafting and revising are used to improve writing competence. The process rather than the product is regarded as the important learning experience.

**Process Instruction:** An emphasis on the 'activity' of a classroom rather than creating a product. A focus on procedures and techniques rather than on learning outcomes, learning 'how to' through inquiry rather than learning through the transmission and memorization of knowledge.

**Productive Bilingualism:** Speaking and writing in the first and second language (as well as listening and reading).

**Productive Language:** Speaking and writing.

**Project Work:** Independent work by an individual student or a group of students often on an interdisciplinary theme. The process of planning, execution, discussion and dialogue, reviewing and reflecting, evaluating and monitoring is an important part of the process. Project work accents co-operative group work and authentic language situations.

**Prosody:** The study of the melody, loudness, speed and rhythm of spoken language; apart from intonation, it includes the transmission of meaning that can be understood from different emphases.

**Psychometric Tests:** Tests to measure an individual's characteristics. The best known psychological tests are IQ tests. Other dispositions are also measured (e.g. attitudes, creativity, skills, dyslexia, personality, needs and motives).

**Pull-Out Program:** Minority language students are taken out of regular, mainstream classrooms for special instruction in the majority language. Special language classes are provided to try to raise a child's level of language in the dominant language of the classroom or of the school.

**Racism:** A system of privilege and penalty based on race. It is based on a belief in the inherent superiority of one race over others, and the maintenance or promotion of economic, social, political and educational differences based on such supposed superiority.

**Readability:** The level of difficulty in a written passage. Readability depends on factors such as length of words, length of sentences, grammatical complexity and word frequency.

**Reception Classes/Centers:** For newly arrived students in a country, to teach the language of the new country, and often the culture.

**Receptive Bilingualism:** Understanding and reading a second language without speaking or writing in that language.

**Receptive Language:** Listening/understanding and reading.

**Register:** (1) A variety of a language closely associated with different contexts in which the language is used (e.g. courtroom, classroom, church) and hence with different people (e.g. police, professor, priest). (2) A variety of a language used by an individual in a certain context.

**Remedial Bilingual Education:** Also known as Compensatory Bilingual Education. Uses the mother tongue only to 'correct' the student's presumed 'deficiency' in the majority language.

**SAIP:** Special Alternative Instructional Programs (USA).

**Scaffolding:** Building on a student's existing repertoire of knowledge and understanding. As the student progresses and becomes more of an independent learner, the help given by teachers can be gradually removed.

**Secondary Bilingualism:** The second language has been formally learnt (see also Primary Bilingualism).

**Second Language:** This term is used in different, overlapping ways, and can mean (1) the second language learnt (chronologically); (2) the weaker language; (3) a language that is not the 'mother tongue'; (4) the less used language. The term is sometimes used to cover third and further languages. The term can also be used to describe a language widely spoken in the country of the learner (as opposed to a foreign language).

**Self-fulfilling Prophecy:** A student is labeled (e.g. by a teacher as having 'limited English'). The label is internalized by the student who behaves in a way that serves to confirm the label. Other people's expectations becoming internalized by a student, for example, and then becoming part of their regular behavior.

**Semantics:** The study of the meaning of language.

**Semilingual:** A controversial term used to describe people whose two languages are both at a low level of development.

**Separate Underlying Proficiency:** The largely discredited idea that two languages exist separately and work independently in the thinking system.

**Sequential Bilingualism:** Bilingualism achieved via learning a second language later than the first language. This is distinct from Simultaneous Bilingualism where two languages are acquired concurrently. When a second language is learnt after the age of three, sequential bilingualism is said to occur.

**Sheltered English:** Content (subject) classes that also include English language development. The curriculum is taught in English in the United States at a comprehensible level to minority language students. The goal of sheltered English is to help minority language students acquire proficiency in English while at the same time achieving well in content areas of the curriculum.

**Sight Vocabulary:** Words which a child can recognize in reading that require no decoding of letters or blends of letters. The instant recognition of basic words.

**Sign Language:** Languages used by many deaf people and by those people who communicate with deaf people that make use of non-verbal communication to communicate meaning. Sign languages are complete languages with their own grammatical systems. Various sign languages have developed in different parts of the world (e.g. American sign language; British sign language; French sign language).

**Silent Way:** A method of second language learning emphasizing independent student learning by means of discovery and problem solving.

**Simultaneous Bilingualism:** Bilingualism achieved via acquiring a first and a second language concurrently. This is distinct from Sequential Bilingualism where the two languages are acquired at different ages. When a second language is learnt before the age of three, simultaneous bilingualism is said to occur.

**Simultaneous Interpreting/Translation:** See Interpreting.

**Skills-based Literacy:** Where the emphasis is on the acquisition of phonics and other language forms, rather than on ways of using those forms.

**SLT:** Second Language Teaching.

**Sociolinguistics:** The study of language in relation to social groups, social class, ethnicity and other interpersonal factors in communication.

**Speech Variety:** A neutral term sometimes used instead of 'dialect' or 'language' where a distinction is difficult.

**Standardization:** The attempt to establish a single standard form of a language particularly in its written form, for official purposes, literature, school curriculum etc.

**Standard Language:** A prestigious variety of a language that has official, formal use (e.g. in government and schooling). A standard language usually has norms for spelling, grammar and vocabulary. The standard variety is often used in literature and other forms of media (e.g. radio, television), in school text books, in centralized policies of the curriculum.

**Standard Variety:** See Standard Language.

**Status Planning:** Language planning which centers on language use and prestige within a region and within particular language domains. See Language Planning.

**Stereotyping:** Classifying members of a group (e.g. a language minority) as if they were all the same. Treating individuals of that group as if no other characteristics of that group were important or existed. Where one characteristic of a group is seen as always associated with other (often negative) characteristics.

**Streaming:** The use of homogeneous groups in teaching (also called tracking, setting, banding, ability grouping).

**Structured Immersion:** The curriculum is taught in English in such programs in the United States at a comprehensible level to minority language students. The goal is to help minority language students acquire proficiency in English while at the same time achieving well in content areas of the curriculum.

**Submersion:** The teaching of minority language pupils solely through the medium of a majority language, often alongside native speakers of the majority language. Minority language pupils are left to sink or swim in the mainstream curriculum.

**Subtractive Bilingualism:** A situation in which a second language is learnt at the expense of the first language, and gradually replaces the first language (e.g. in-migrants to a country or minority language pupils in submersion education).

**SUP:** see Separate Underlying Proficiency.

**Syntax:** The study of how words combine into sentences. Rules governing the ways words are combined and organized.

**Target Language:** A second or foreign language being learned or taught.

**TBE:** Transitional Bilingual Education. Temporary use of the child's home language in the classroom, leading to only the majority language being allowed in classroom instruction. (See Early-Exit/Late-Exit Bilingual Education Programs).

**Teacher Talk:** A variety of communication used by teachers in classrooms. Teacher talk is specific to the needs of instruction and classroom management, sometimes simplified as in foreigner talk.

**TEFL:** Teaching English as a Foreign Language.

**Territorial Principle:** A claim to the right to a language within a territory. The right to use a language within a geographical area.

**TESFL:** Teaching English as a Second and a Foreign Language.

**TESL:** Teaching English as a Second Language.

**TESOL:** (1) Teachers of English to Speakers of Other Languages. (2) Teaching English as a Second or Other Language.

**Threshold Level:** (1) A level of language competence a person has to reach to gain cognitive benefits from owning two languages. (2) The Threshold Level is used by the Council of Europe to define a minimal level of language proficiency needed to function in a foreign language. Various contexts are specified where languages are used and students are expected to reach specific objectives to attain the threshold level.

**Title VII: The Bilingual Education Act:** Title VII of the Elementary and Secondary Education Act of 1968, established US federal policy for bilingual education for language minority students. Reauthorized in 1994 as part of the Improving America's Schools Act, Title VII's new provisions increased the state role and aided applicants seeking to develop bilingual proficiency.

**Total Communication:** A method of teaching deaf and hearing impaired children based on the use of both sign language and spoken language.

**Tracking:** The use of homogeneous ability groups in teaching (also called setting, streaming, banding, ability grouping).

**Trade Language:** A language that is adopted or evolves as a medium of communication in business or commerce between different language groups. Many pidgins evolved as trade languages in ports or centers of commerce.

**Transfer:** See Language Transfer.

**Transitional Bilingual Education (TBE):** The primary purpose of these US programs is to facilitate a student's transition to an all-English instructional environment while initially using the native language in the classroom. Transitional bilingual education programs vary in the amount of native language instruction provided and the duration of the program.

**Two-Way Programs:** Also known as Developmental Bilingual Education, Two-Way Dual Language Programs and Two-Way Bilingual/Immersion Programs. Two languages are used for approximately equal time in the curriculum. Classrooms have a mixture of native speakers of each language.

**Unmarked Language:** A majority language distinct from a minority language, and usually highly valued in society.

**US English:** An organization committed to making English the official language of the United States.

**Vernacular:** A indigenous or heritage language of an individual or community. A vernacular language is used to define a native language as opposed to (1) a classical language such as Latin and Greek, (2) an internationally used language such as English and French, (3) the official or national language of a country.

**Whole Language Approach:** An amorphous cluster of ideas about language development in the classroom. The approach is against basal readers and phonics in learning to read. Generally the approach supports an holistic and integrated learning of reading, writing, spelling and oracy. The language used must have relevance and meaning to the child. Language development engages co-operative sharing and cultivates empowerment. The use of language for communication is stressed; the function rather than the form of language.

**Withdrawal Classes:** Also known as 'pull-out' classes. Children are taken out of an ordinary class for special instruction.

**Writing Conference:** The teacher and the student discuss the writing the student is to complete, the process of composing. The teacher plans regular discussions with individual students about their writing to promote personal awareness of their style, content, confidence and communication of ideas.

**Zone of Proximal Development:** New areas of learning within a student's reach. Vygotsky saw the zone of proximal development as the distance between a student's level of development as revealed when problem solving without adult help, and the level of potential development as determined by a student problem solving in collaboration with peers or teachers. The zone of proximal development is where new understandings are possible through collaborative interaction and inquiry.

## Acknowledgement

The author wishes to thank Colin Baker for allowing me to use this glossary from his book *A Parents' and Teachers' Guide to Bilingualism* (Baker, 1995). Professor Ofelia García and Dr Sylvia Prys Jones also contributed to this glossary.

# Further Reading

Baker, C. (2000) *The Care and Education of Young Bilinguals.* Clevedon: Multilingual Matters.

Brutt-Griffler, J. (2002) *Bilingual Education and Bilingualism.* Clevedon: Multilingual Matters.

Carder, M.W. (1993) Are we creating biliterate bilinguals? *International Schools Journal* 26, 19–27. Saxmundham: Peridot Press, a division of John Catt Educational Ltd.

Carder, M.W. (2002) ESL students in the IB Middle Years Programme. *ECIS: International Schools Magazine* 5 (1), 22. Saxmundham: Peridot Press, a division of John Catt Educational Ltd.

Carder, M.W. (2002) Intercultural awareness, bilingualism, and ESL in the International Baccalaureate, with particular reference to the MYP. *The International Schools Journal* 21 (2) 34–41. Saxmundham: Peridot Press, a division of John Catt Educational Ltd.

Carder, M.W. (2005) Bilingualism and the Council of International Schools. *International Schools Journal* 24 (2), 19–27. Saxmundham: Peridot Press, a division of John Catt Educational Ltd.

Chamot, A.U. and O'Malley, J.M. (1994) *A Cognitive Academic Language Learning Approach: An ESL Content-based Curriculum.* New York: Longman.

Cloud, N., Genesee, F. and Hamayan, E. (2000) *Dual Language Instruction.* Boston: Heinle & Heinle.

Collier, V. and Ovando, C. (1998) *Bilingual and ESL Classrooms* (2nd edn). Boston: McGraw-Hill.

Collier, V. and Thomas, W. (1999) Making US schools effective for English language learners Part 1. *TESOL Matters* 9 (4), 1–6.

Crystal, D. (1997) *English as a Global Language.* Cambridge: Cambridge University Press.

Cummins, J. (1978) The cognitive development of children in immersion programmes. *The Canadian Modern Languages Review* 34, 855–883.

Cummins, J. (1981) The role of primary language development in promoting educational success for language minority students. In California State Department of Education (ed.) *Schooling and Language Minority Students: A Theoretical Framework* (pp. 3–49). Los Angeles: Evaluation Dissemination and Assessment Center, California State University.

Cummins, J. (1984) *Bilingualism and Special Education: Issues in Assessment and Pedagogy.* Clevedon: Multilingual Matters.

Cummins, J. (1986) Empowering minority students: A framework for intervention. *Harvard Educational Review* 56 (1), 18–36.

Cummins, J. (1989) *Empowering Minority Students.* Sacramento, CA: California Association for Bilingual Education (CABE).

Cummins, J. (1991) Interdependence of first- and second-language proficiency in bilingual children. In E. Bialystok (ed.) *Language Processing in Bilingual Children* (pp. 70–89). Cambridge: Cambridge University Press.

Cummins, J. (1999) Beyond adversarial discourse: Searching for common ground in the education of bilingual students. In C. Ovando and P. McLaren (eds) *The Politics of Multiculturalism and Bilingual Education: Students and Teachers Caught in the Cross Fire* (pp. 126–147). Boston: McGraw Hill.

Delpit, L.D. (1988) The silenced dialogue: Power and pedagogy in educating other people's children. *Harvard Educational Review* 58 (3), 280–298.

Freeman, Y.S. and Freeman, D.E. (1992) *Whole Language for Second Language Learners.* Portsmouth, NH: Heinemann.

Gallagher, E. (2001) Foreign language learning in early childhood. *International Schools Journal* 20 (2), 54–56. Saxmundham: Peridot Press, a division of John Catt Educational Ltd.

Gallagher, E. (2002) Bilingual is best. *The International Educator* 16 (4), 25. Cummaquid, MA: Overseas Schools Assistance Corp.

Gallagher, E. (2002) Passports to better understanding. *ECIS: International Schools Magazine* 4 (2) 28. Saxmundham: Peridot Press, a division of John Catt Educational Ltd.

Gallagher, E. (2003) The key role of the administrator in the success of the ESL programme. *International Schools Journal* 22 (2), 9–11. Saxmundham: Peridot Press, a division of John Catt Educational Ltd.

Genesee, F. (1987) *Learning through Two Languages: Studies of Immersion and Bilingual Education.* New York: Newbury House.

Genesee, F. (ed.) (1994) *Educating Second Language Children: The Whole Child, the Whole Curriculum, the Whole Community.* Cambridge: Cambridge University Press.

Giroux, H.A. (1993) *Living Dangerously Multiculturalism and the Politics of Difference.* New York: Peter Lang.

Graddol, D. (1997) *The Future of English?* London: British Council.

Hakuta, K. (1986) *Mirror of Language: The Debate on Bilingualism.* New York: Basic Books.

Halliday, M. (1994) *An Introduction to Functional Grammar* (2nd edn). London: Edward Arnold.

IBO (2007) *Making the P.Y.P. Happen: A Curriculum Framework for International Primary Education.* Geneva: IBO.

Krashen, S. (1999) *Condemned Without a Trial: Bogus Arguments Against Bilingual Education.* Portsmouth, NH: Heinemann.

Krashen, S. (2003) *Explorations in Language Acquisition and Use.* Portsmouth, NH: Heinemann.

Krashen, S. (2006) *English Fever.* Taipei: Crane publishing Co., Ltd.

Lambert, W. (1978) Cognitive and socio-cultural consequences of bilingualism. *The Canadian Modern Languages Review* 34, 537–547.

Lo Bianco, J. and Freebody, P. (1997) Australian literacies: Informing national policy on literacy education. A commissioned discussion paper for The Minister for Employment, Education, Training and Youth Affairs. Canberra: Language Australia.

Murphy, E. (ed.) (1990) *ESL: A Handbook for Teachers and Administrators in International Schools.* Clevedon: Multilingual Matters.

Murphy, E. (ed.) (2003) Editor's preface. *The International Schools Compendium* 1. Saxmundham: Peridot Press, a division of John Catt Educational Ltd.

Murphy, E. (2003) Monolingual international schools and the young non-English-speaking child. *Journal of Research in International Education* 2 (1), 9–10. Saxmundham: Peridot Press, a division of John Catt Educational Ltd.

Polias, J. (2003) *ESL Scope and Scales.* Hindmarsh, South Australia: Department of Education and Children's Services.

Sears, C. (1998) *Second Language Students in Mainstream Classrooms.* Clevedon: Multilingual Matters.

Skutnabb-Kangas, T. (1984) *Bilingualism or Not – the Education of Minorities.* Clevedon: Multilingual Matters.

Skutnabb-Kangas, T. (ed.) (1995) *Multilingualism for All.* Lisse, The Netherlands: Swets and Zeitlinger.

Skutnabb-Kangas, T. (2000) *Linguistic Genocide in Education – or Worldwide Diversity and Human Rights?* London: Lawrence Erlbaum Associates.

Skutnabb-Kangas, T. and Toukomaa, P. (1976) *Teaching Migrant Children's Mother Tongue and Learning the Language of the Host Country in the Context of the Socio-cultural Situation of the Migrant Family.* Helsinki, Finland: The Finnish National Commission for UNESCO.

Skutnabb-Kangas, T. and Toukomaa, P. (1977) *The Intensive Teaching of the Mother Tongue to Migrant Children of Pre-school Age and Children in the Lower Level of Comprehensive School.* Helsinki, Finland: The Finnish National Commission for UNESCO.

Spolsky, B. (ed.) (1999) *Concise Encyclopaedia of Educational Linguistics*. Oxford: Elsevier Science Ltd.

Vygotsky, L.S. (1962) *Thought and Language*. Cambridge, MA: Harvard University Press.

Wong Fillmore, L. and Valadez, C. (1986) Teaching bilingual learners. In M.C. Wittrock (ed.) *Handbook of Research on Teaching* (3rd edn) (pp. 648–685). New York: Macmillan.

# References

Ada, A.F. (1988a) The Pajaro Valley experience: Working with Spanish speaking parents to develop children's reading and writing skills in the home through the use of children's literature. In T. Skutnabb-Kangas and J. Cummins (eds) *Minority Education: From Shame to Struggle* (pp. 223–238). Clevedon: Multilingual Matters.

Ada, A.F. (1988b) Creative reading: A relevant methodology for language minority children. In L.M. Malave (ed.) *NABE'87 Theory, Research and Application: Selected Papers* (pp. 97–112). Buffalo, NY: State University of New York.

Alexander, S. and Baker, K. (1992) Some ethical issues in applied social psychology: The case of bilingual education and self-esteem. *Journal of Applied Social Psychology* 22, 1741–1757.

Allan, M.J. (2002) Making schools multicultural. ECIS conference paper first presented at ECIS Annual Conference, Berlin, November 2002.

Allan, M.J. (2003) Frontier crossing. *Journal of Research in International Education* JRIE 2 (1), 83–110. London: Sage Publications Ltd.

Allen, P., Swain, M., Harley, B. and Cummins, J. (1990) Aspects of classroom treatment: Towards a more comprehensive view of second language education. In B. Harley, P. Allen, J. Cummins and M. Swain (eds) *The Development of Second Language Proficiency* (pp. 57–81). Cambridge: Cambridge University Press

Baker, C. (1995) *A Parents' and Teachers' Guide to Bilingualism*. Clevedon: Multilingual Matters.

Baker, C. (2003) *Foundations of Bilingual Education and Bilingualism* (3rd edn). Clevedon: Multilingual Matters.

Baker, C. and Pry Jones, S. (1998) (eds) *Encyclopaedia of Bilingualism and Bilingual Education*. Clevedon: Multilingual Matters.

Bransford, J.D., Brown A. L. and Cocking, R.R. (2000) (eds) *How People Learn: Brain, Mind Experience and School*. Washington, DC: National Academic Press.

Burgess, A. (1964) *Language Maid Plane*. London: Hodder and Stoughton.

Burke, D. (1998) Inclusive curriculum and learners from non English speaking backgrounds. In *ESL in the Mainstream Teacher Development Course*. South Australia: DETE Publishing.

CAL (Center for Applied Linguistics) (2000) Cueing systems. In *Enhancing English Language Learning in Elementary Classrooms Study Guide*. McHenry, IL: Delta Systems Co., Inc.

Carder, M.W. (2007) *Bilingualism in International Schools*. Clevedon: Multilingual Matters.

Chamot, A.U. (1992) Changing instruction for language minority students to achieve national goals. Presented at *Third National Research Symposium on Limited English Proficient Student Issues*. Online document at http://www.ncela.gwu.edu/pubs/symposia/third/chamot.htm (accessed January 2008).

Collier, V. (2003) Foreword. In Edna Murphy (ed.) *The International Schools Journal Compendium*, Volume 1. ESL. Saxmundham: Peridot Press, a division of John Catt Educational Ltd.

Collier, V. and Thomas, W. (1997) School effectiveness for language minority students. *NCBE Resource Collection* 9. Washington, DC: NCBE The George Washington University, Center for the Study of Language Education. Online document at http://www.ncela.gwu.edu/pubs/resource/effectiveness/thomas-collier97.pdf (accessed January 2008).

Corson, D. (2001) *Language Diversity and Education*. Mahwah, NJ: Lawrence Erlbaum Associates, Inc.

Cummins, J. (1981) Age on arrival and immigrant second language learning in Canada: A reassessment. *Applied Linguistics* 2, 132–149.

Cummins, J. (2000) Immersion education for the millennium: What we have learned from 30 years of research on second language immersion. Online document at http://www.iteachil-earn.com/cummins/immersion2000.html (accessed January 2008).

Cummins, J. (2001a) Quoted in C. Baker and N.H. Hornberger (eds) *An Introductory Reader to the Writings of Jim Cummins*. Clevedon: Multilingual Matters.

Cummins, J. (2001b) *Negotiating Identities: Education for Empowerment in a Diverse Society*. Los Angeles: California Association for Bilingual Education.

Cummins, J. (2004) *Language, Power and Pedagogy*. Clevedon: Multilingual Matters.

Daniels, H. (2002) *Literature Circles Voice and Choice in Book Clubs and Reading Groups*. Markham, Ontario: Stenhouse Publishers.

DECS (South Australian Department of Education and Children's Services) (1999) *ESL in the Mainstream*. Hindmarsh, South Australia: Department of Education and Children's Services.

Early, M., Cummins, J. and Willinsky, J. (2002) From literacy to multiliteracies: Designing learning environments for knowledge generation within the new economy. Proposal funded by the Social Sciences and Humanities Research Council of Canada.

Edwards, V. (1995) *Reading in Multilingual Classrooms*. Reading: Reading and Language Information Centre, University of Reading.

Foertsch, M. (1992) *Reading In and Out of School*. Washington, DC: US Department of Education.

Freire, P. (1983) Banking education. In H. Giroux and D. Purpel (eds) *The Hidden Curriculum and Moral Education: Deception or Discovery?* Berkeley, CA: McCutcheon Publishing Corporation.

Freire, P. and Macedo, D. (1987) *Literacy: Reading the Word and the World*. South Hadley, MA: Bergen and Garvey.

Gallagher, E. (2002) Back to the mother-tongue. *ECIS: International Schools Magazine* 5 (1), 20–21. Saxmundham: Peridot Press, a division of John Catt Educational Ltd.

Gallagher, E. (2003) What's in a name? *ECIS: International Schools Magazine* 6 (1), 12. Saxmundham: Peridot Press, a division of John Catt Educational Ltd.

Gallagher, E. (2005) Comment. *ECIS: International Schools Magazine* 8 (1), 3–4. Saxmundham: Peridot Press, a division of John Catt Educational Ltd.

Gallagher, E. (2007) A curriculum for the whole child. *ECIS: International Schools Magazine* 9 (3) 18–19. Saxmundham: Peridot Press, a division of John Catt Educational Ltd.

Garcia, O., Skutnabb-Kangas, T. and Torres Guzman M.E. (2006) *Imagining Multilingual Schools*. Clevedon: Multilingual Matters.

Gibbons, P. (1995) Learning a new register in a second language: The role teacher/student talk (Working Paper No. 1). Sydney: University of Technology.

Gibbons, P. (1998) Classroom talk and the learning of new registers in a second language. *Language and Education* 12 (2), 99–118.

Gibbons, P. (2002) *Scaffolding Language, Scaffolding Learning: Teaching Second Language Learners in the Mainstream Classroom*. Portsmouth, NH: Heinemann.

Giroux, H.A. (1991) Series introduction: Rethinking the pedagogy of voice difference and cultural struggle. In E. Walsh (ed.) *Pedagogy and the Struggle for Voice: Issues of Language, Power, and Schooling for Puerto Ricans* (pp. XV-XXVII). Toronto: OISE Press.

Giroux, H.A. (1994) *Disturbing Pleasures: Learning Popular Culture*. New York: Routledge.

Hakuta, K., Butler, Y.G. and Witt, D. (2000) *How Long Does it Take English Learners to Attain Proficiency?* Santa Barbara, CA: University of California Linguistic Minority Research Institute.

Halliday, M. (1975) *Learning How to Mean: Explorations in the Development of Language*. London: Arnold.

Harley, B., Allen, P., Cummins, J. and Swain, M. (1990) (eds) *The Development of Second Language Proficiency*. Cambridge: Cambridge University Press.

Hayden, M. (2001) International education and the IB programmes. Paper presented to a meeting of the IBO Academic Advisory Committee, April, Geneva.

Haywood, T. (2002) An international dimension to management and leadership skills for international education. In M. Hayden, J. Thompson and G. Walker (eds) *International Education in Practice* (pp. 170–184). London: Kogan Page.

Hill, I. (2002) The history of international education: An international baccalaureate perspective. In M. Hayden, J. Thompson and G. Walker (eds) *International Education in Practice* (pp. 18–29). London: Kogan Page.

Hopkins, D., Ainscow, M. and West, M. (1994) *School Improvement in an Era of Change*. London: Cassell.

IBO (1996) *Mission Statement*. Geneva: IBO.

IBO (2002a) *Schools Guide to PYP*. Geneva: IBO.

IBO (2002b) *A Basis for Practice: The Diploma Programme*. Geneva: IBO.

IBO (2004) *Middle Years Programme Second Language and Mother-tongue Development: A Guide for Schools*. Geneva: IBO.

IBO (2006) *IB Learner Profile Booklet*. Geneva: IBO. Online document at http://www.ibo.org/heads/newheads/documents/learnerprofileEng.pdf (accessed January 2008).

Jameson, J. (1999) Issues in grading limited English proficient students. *From Theory to Practice*, No. 9. Tampa, FL: The Region XIV Comprehensive Center at ETS.

Klesmer, H. (1994) Assessment and teacher perceptions of esl student achievement. *English Quarterly* 26 (3), 8–11.

Krashen, S. (2004) *The Power of Reading* (2nd edn). Englewood, CO: Libraries Unlimited Inc.

Krashen, S. and Biber, D. (1988) *On Course: Bilingual Education Success in California*. Sacramento, CA: California Association for Bilingual Education.

Krashen, S. and Terrell, T. (1983) *The Natural Approach: Language Acquisition in the Classroom*. Oxford: Pergamon.

McCaig, N. (1992) Birth of a notion. *The Global Nomad Quarterly* 1 (1), 1–2.

Moll, L.C., Amanti, C., Neff, D. and Gonzales, N. (1992) Funds of knowledge using a qualitative approach to connect homes and classrooms. *Theory into Practice* 31 (2), 132–141.

Murphy, E. (ed.) (2003) It's about time . . . . *International Schools Journal* 22 (2), 5–8. Saxmundham: Peridot Press, a division of John Catt Educational Ltd.

Nagy, W., Anderson, R. and Herman, P. (1985) Learning words from context. *Reading Research Quarterly* 20 (2), 233–253.

Orellano Benado, M.E. (1998) Pluralism and the ethics of Internationalism. *IB World* 17, 11–12.

Pollock, D.C. and van Reken R.E. (2001) *Third Culture Kids*. London: Nicholas Brealey Publishing/Intercultural Press.

Poplin, M. and Weres, J. (1992) *Voices from the Inside: A Report on Schooling from Inside the Classroom*. Claremont, CA: The Institute for Education in Transformation at the Claremont Graduate School.

Rader, D. and Sittig, L.H. (2003) *New Kid in School: Using Literature to Help Children in Transition*. New York: Teachers College Press.

Ramirez, J.D., Yuen, S.D. and Ramey, D.R. (1991) Executive summary, final report: longitudinal study of structured immersion strategy early exit and late transitional bilingual education program for language minority children (contract no. 300-87-0156). Washington, DC: US Department of Education.

Ruiz, R. (1984) Orientations in language planning. *National Association for Bilingual Education (NABE) Journal* 8 (2), 15–34.

Skelton, M. (2002) Defining 'international' in an international curriculum. In M. Hayden, J. Thompson and G. Walker (eds) *International Education in Practice* (pp. 39–54). London: Kogan Page.

Sousa, D.A. (1998) Is the fuss about brain research justified? *Education Week* 18 (16), 35.

Swain, M. (1995) Three functions of output in second language learning. In G. Cook and B. Seidlhofer (eds) *Principle and Practice in Applied Linguistics: Studies in Honour of H.G. Widdowson.* Oxford: Oxford University Press.

Useem, R.H. (1976) Third culture kids. *Today's Education* 65 (3), 103–105.

van Ek, J.A. (1975) *The Threshold Level in a European Unit: Credit System for Modern Language Learning by Adults.* Council of Europe (reprinted 1980 Pergamon Press).

Vygotsky, L.S. (1978) *Mind in Society: The Development of Higher Psychological Processes.* London: Harvard University Press.

Wong Fillmore, L. (1991) When learning a second language means losing the first. *Early Childhood Research Quarterly* 6, 323–344.

# Index

Accreditation, 4, 7, 11, 17, 19-25, 29, 34, 91, 109, 115
ACER *See* Australian Council of Educational Research
Ada, A.F., 21-23, 34, 49-51, 58
ADAPT model, 70-72
Additive bilingualism, 2, 5, 25-26, 81, 85, 91, 107, 132
Advanced Placement (AP) exam, 130
Affective Filter Theory, 46, 61
Allan, M., 19-20
Applied Linguistics, 2, 113
Asia, 16
Assessment / testing
– External examinations, 130-131
– For placement, 121-123
– For special needs, 132
– In the mainstream, 126-128
– Interpreting results of, 13, 36, 112, 123-125
– Iowa Test of Basic Skills, 117
– IQ tests, 122
– Methods for, 128
– Policy for, 9, 99, 106, 117, 121-125
– Standard tests, 11, 34, 116-117, 130
– Using the L1, 4, 34, 122
Assimilation, 3
Australia, 1, 24, 63
Australian Council of Educational Research (ACER), 117

Baker, C., 2-4, 37-39, 62, 84, 111
Bartlett, K., 31, 63
Biber, D., 48
BICS and CALP, 35-39, 113
Bilingualism, 2-5, 38, 62, 80-81, 85, 109
Biliteracy, 4, 16, 105
Brain research, 35, 43-46
Bransford, J.D., 93, 103
Burgess, A., 92
Burke, D., 77, 107

CAL *See* Center for Applied Linguistics
CALP *See* BICS and CALP
Canada, 1, 42, 93, 114
Carder, M.W., 53, 62
CAS *See* Creative Action Service

Center for Applied Linguistics (CAL), 55
Centre National d'Enseignement à Distance (CNED), 120
Chamot, A.U., 103
Child Centred Learning *See* Progressive Pedagogy
CIE *See* University of Cambridge International Examinations
CIS *See* Council of International Schools
Class size, 106, 109, 118
CNED *See* Centre National d'Enseignement à Distance
Cohen, S., 93
Collier, V., 1-2, 25, 35, 59-62, 94, 120
Common Underlying Proficiency (CUP), 38-39
Communicative methodology, 45
Comprehensible input, 47-49
Context embedded communication, 40
Corson, D., 9, 16, 82
Council of Europe, 3, 45
Council of International Schools (CIS), 16, 25, 29-30, 33, 95, 105
Creative Action Service (CAS), 27-28
Critical inquiry, 13-15, 18
Critical literacy, 15-16, 20-22, 34
Critical thinking, 13, 18, 84, 130
Cummins, J.
– On academic language learning, 48-51
– On BICS & CALP, 35-38, 113
– On bilingualism, 2, 8
– On common underlying proficiency, 38-39
– On context embedded communication, 40-41
– On critical literacy, 21-23
– On dominant / dominated cultures, 77-78, 82
– On dual language identity texts, 93-94, 97
– On genre, 52
– On importance of the L1, 62, 95, 119
– On parents as partners, 77
– On reading skills, 54
– On relations of power, 5-12
– On traditional pedagogy, 15
– On transformative pedagogy, 15, 24
CUP *See* Common Underlying Proficiency

Danesi, M., 62